SECRETS OF THE HAND-

YOUR PAST, PRESENT AND FUTURE

SECRETS OF THE HAND-

YOUR PAST, PRESENT AND FUTURE

BY

CHEIRO

GYAN

Published by

Gyan Publishing House
5, Ansari Road
Daryaganj, New Delhi-110002
Phone: 011-47034999, 9811692060
E-mail: books@gyanbooks.com

Distribution Network
gyanbooks.com
India, USA, Canada, UK, Australia

ISBN: 978-93-6280-677-2 (PB)
First Published, 1924

2nd Impression 2024

Printed at: Gyan Press, Delhi.

SECRETS OF THE HAND-YOUR PAST, PRESENT AND FUTURE
Author: CHEIRO

SECRETS OF THE HAND

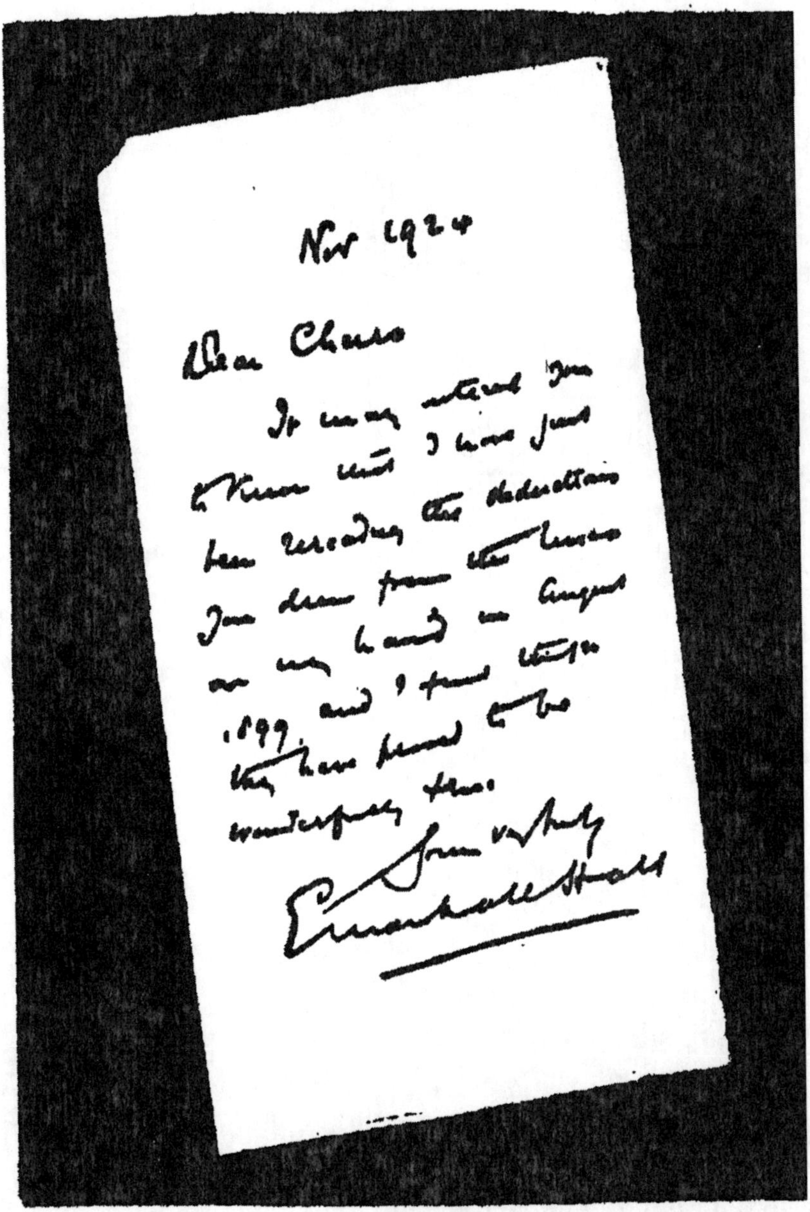

Nov 1924

Dear Cheiro

It may interest you to know that I have just been rereading the deductions you drew from the lines on my hand in August 1899, and I find that they have proved to be wonderfully true.

Yours very truly
E Marshall Hall

A Letter from
the late Sir Edward Marshall Hall, K.C.

SECRETS OF THE HAND—

YOUR PAST, PRESENT, AND FUTURE

BY

CHEIRO

WITH SIXTY-EIGHT ILLUSTRATIONS.

HERBERT JENKINS LIMITED
3 YORK STREET, LONDON, S.W.1

CONTENTS

ILLUSTRATIONS

PUBLISHERS' PREFACE

"CHEIRO," the greatest and the most successful reader of hands in the history of the world, after twenty years of continuous work, retired from public life and no one will be able to consult him again.

Believing, as he proved for years, in the advantage all classes would have in being able to know their faults, their weak points and their true character, "Cheiro" has at last been persuaded to teach the secrets of his wonderful art by means of the Cinema, and to give to the world a low-priced book within the reach of all, whereby any person of average intelligence may be able to understand the meaning of the lines and marks in their own hands, to read their past, present, and indications of their future, and by so doing they may be enabled to avoid evils and make the best out of themselves, their opportunities and their characters, and thus realise the truth of that famous Greek proverb, "Know Thyself."

Opportunity never knocks twice at one's door, therefore, the man or woman is doubly armed in the battle of life who can tell *when the opportunity will come.*

In the following pages, "Cheiro" puts clearly and distinctly and in simple language the meaning of all those markings on the hand, which he had proved by his long experience bear out his theories, and no one can read this book without being able to realise what the "Book of Fate" contains for themselves.

WHO "CHEIRO" IS

The name "Cheiro" covers one of the most remarkable personalities of modern times, a highly-gifted man who, had he desired, might have won fame in many other pursuits in life, but who chose at the very threshold of his manhood to live in the East, so that he might be able to study the forgotten wisdom of those wonderful races such as the Hindus, the Chinese and Persians, and returning to Western civilisation he took a sacred vow that for twenty years he would devote himself to converting the most intellectual and highest personages in the world to believe in the strange Science of which he had made himself the Master.

In carrying out his vow his success has been phenomenal. He has read and taken impressions of the hands of most of the crowned heads of Europe, together with Presidents of Republics and Kings of Commerce. One and all have borne witness that "Cheiro's" powers of predicting events years in advance from the lines in their hands have been something akin to marvellous.

Taking one or two illustrations at random:—"Cheiro" predicted the date of Queen Victoria's death, the exact year and even the month when King Edward VII would pass away, the terrible destiny that awaited the late Czar of Russia, the assassination of King Humbert of Italy, the attempt on the Shah's life in Paris, and in thousands of well-known persons' lives, with equal accuracy, the leading events of their careers.

It is on record that one of the most dramatic predictions ever made, was when in 1894 (twenty-two years before the tragic event) "Cheiro" foretold to Lord Kitchener the exact year of his death—and *the likely form it would take.* The words of this remarkable prediction made by "Cheiro" at the War Office, were the following:

"That he, Kitchener, would meet his death in his sixty-sixth year—not the end that a Soldier might naturally expect on the battlefield—but that his death would be caused by water, most probably by storm or disaster at Sea, with the attendant chance of some form of capture by an enemy and exile from which he would never recover."

When this prediction was made, the great Kitchener was only a plain Colonel and in that year 1894 he gave "Cheiro" a signed impression of his hand which had strangely enough the Seal of the War Office imprinted on it, which may be seen at the top of the second finger in the Film reproduction of Kitchener's hand, which has been shown at all the principal Cinemas in England.

Lord Kitchener never forgot this prediction. During the Great War, while at the Front, as related in the Press, he mentioned it to General de Ballincourt and members of his Staff.

The tragic sinking of the battleship "Hampshire" on the evening of the 5th June, 1916, *in Lord Kitchener's sixty-sixth year*, and the chance that the great Soldier might have been captured by an enemy submarine, bore out "Cheiro's" prediction to the letter, and is a remarkable example of the accuracy of his system in reading the lines of the hand.

A similar prediction was made by "Cheiro" to the celebrated journalist, W. T. Stead, and with equal exactness, when he went to his death in the disaster to the "Titanic" on her first voyage.

It can be said without exaggeration, that "Cheiro"

has become world-famous through the perfection to which he has brought this Study of the Hand. In London, Paris, New York, Boston, Chicago, in all the great towns of America, in Leningrad, Rome and the principal Continental cities, he has demonstrated that the lines of the hand are a veritable chart of life, his success has been certified to by all classes and in his Visitors' Book autographed testimonies may be seen that are *without a parallel* in the history of the World.

In this small but concise work that we now issue to the public, the reader will find clearly drawn illustrations of the various lines that seem so bewildering when glanced at in ignorance of their real meaning. The Author, however, illuminates the whole subject in a lucid style peculiarly his own, and in such a form that the reader can "Know Himself" or Herself, in a way that would be impossible by any other study.

We have no hesitation in saying that this book places in concise form rare knowledge that cannot but be found of benefit to all.

THE PUBLISHERS.

"CHEIRO'S" FOREWORD

THE HISTORY OF THE STUDY OF THE HAND

DEAR READER,

I suggest that we sit down together—just we two—and that you let me tell you, in plain simple English, a few facts that you have most probably never heard of before about this fascinating Study of the Hand.

In your case you have been too occupied, very likely, in learning all those things that were necessary for you to learn so that you were able to earn your living, or having earned it, to continue to hold your own in the world of men.

In my case, on the contrary, I have been placed in a position of being able to concentrate my mind on this strange study of life from a very early age. From then to my twentieth year, I studied all the literature I could obtain on the subject. I travelled to countries such as India—the cradle of occult knowledge—and lastly, in obedience to a vow I took—for the twenty years following—I made a professional career out of this Study, reading from morning till night the hands of all sorts and conditions of men, women and children in all parts of the world.

In my case, therefore, I *ought* to know something about this subject, and I *should* be able to impart a great deal of that knowledge to you.

Let me try and do so—and I assure you, if you will only try and follow what I am prepared to put before you, that there is no study you can take up that will prove more fascinating, or one that *will reward you more.*

In the first place, you will gain a knowledge of yourself that is beyond all money value; you will gain a knowledge of others that will place you in a position of superiority over them; and, further, by your knowledge you will become the centre of attraction in whatever town, city or community you may happen to live in.

Is there any other study that can place you in such a position?

Let us consider for a few moments the History of this Study—see where it came from, who were the races that believed in it, and what status have the men and women who follow its warnings and advice even in the present day.

You never thought it had a history! I can hear you say. You thought it was only believed in by superstitious people—practised by travelling gipsies from door to door, and so on.

You only thought all that, my dear Reader, simply because *you did not know*.

Will you be surprised to hear—and what I am going to tell you is, on my word of honour, *true*, and can be verified by you if you have the time to do it—that this Study I am going to teach you *is as old as language itself?*

In the far-off dawn of civilisation, history informs us that the *first evidence of a word language* belongs to the Aryan race.

To their descendants, the ancient Hindus, we owe the discovery of the precession of the equinoxes, which takes place every 25,600 years, and we, with all the marvellous scientific instruments at our disposal, have only in recent years proved *their calculations to be correct*.

The intellectual power that was able to make such a discovery speaks for itself, and it is to *this self-same people* that we can trace the origin of the Study of the Hand.

In that far distant age, the greatest study of mankind was: MAN. The Hindus discovered that Man was the epitome of the entire universe—the veritable Son of God: everything was created for him and for his use, and so by the study of Man they came to "know God," and through Man understood the Works of God.

With their marvellous knowledge of the Heavens at their disposal, and observations handed down for thousands of years, they created the science of Astrology and "Fadic" numbers, and traced the influence of the Planetary System in men's lives.

Their observations on the character of each individual, their diseases, their destiny as shown by the signs of the Zodiac at birth have been handed down to us from the ages, and, like their calculations as to the precession of the equinoxes, have not been found wrong.

In connection with this study of Mankind, the ancient Hindus first studied the lines and marks found on all parts of the human body: this they called the Study of Samudrika; or the Study of the Lines of the Body.

From this they created: Hastrika—the Study of the Lines of the Hand, or the epitome of the Study of Samudrika.

The period of Time when these studies were created by the Hindus was long before the dawn of civilisation had reached nations we now call ancient; a period long before Persia or Egypt had been heard of; before Abraham the Father of the Hebrews had been born, and consequently before even the Ten Commandments, which we obey, were given to Moses.

From the ancient Hindus the Study of the Hand can be traced through the distant civilisations of China, Tibet, Persia, Egypt and finally to Greece, where it was honoured and taught by some of the great Greek philosophers.

Anaxagoras taught this study to his pupils and practised it about the year 440 B.C.

Hispanus sent a book on Cheiromancy, as it was then called, *written in gold letters*, to Alexander the Great as "a study worthy the attention of an elevated and enquiring mind."

It was also sanctioned and studied by such great men as Aristotle, Pliny, Paracelsus, Cardamis, the Emperor Augustus and others of note.

Further it is related by Josephus, the Historian of the Jews, that Cæsar was so well versed in this study that "one day a so-called son of Herod had audience with him, and he at once detected the impostor *because his hand was destitute of all marks of royalty.*"

During the terrible wars that followed the break-up of the Roman Empire, the Study we are considering, like many other arts and sciences, became lost, or, if not lost, covered with superstition, and fell into the hands of travelling bands of gipsies and nomads that roamed over Europe.

In 1475, one of the first books printed in movable type following the Bible, was a work on this subject in German, called "Die Kunst Ciromanta," and in 1490 another called "Cyromantia Aristotelis cum Figuris," which to-day may be seen in the British Museum.

From the Continent the Study of the Hand spread into Britain and had such power that Henry VIII made a law forbidding it to be taught or practised. Perhaps the "much married monarch," if the truth were known, was afraid his numerous wives would have found out their fate too easily by the aid of this study!

Strange as it may seem, his daughter Queen Elizabeth encouraged the art, and it is on record that Dr. John Dee became her Royal Palmist and Astrologer and that she consulted him on all occasions when troubled over affairs of State.

It is further on record that one day when reading her hand, the old Palmist warned her of the invasion of the Spanish Armada and the Queen, acting on his advice, had the "fire ships" built that routed the monster galleons of Spain.

England may perhaps owe her greatness to this study—who can tell?

The greatest opposition to the practice and cultivation of all occult studies has come from "the Church." I mean by this no particular creed or sect, but "the Church" in any shape or form as a body.

Individually there are clergymen and priests of every denomination who believe in this Study as an accurate means of knowing character and interpreting the tendencies, inherent or otherwise, that may affect the future of the individual. During my career hundreds of my clients were representatives of one Church or another. In London, the celebrated Father Vaughan, after his visit to me, wrote: "God bless you. Be a sower as well as a reaper." His characteristic words and signature lie before me as I write.

The recent Bishop of Birmingham wrote in my Autograph Book:

"To 'Cheiro.'

The past quite accurate—may you prove right as to the future.—Many thanks for your clear statements and charming way of telling the tale of life."

(*Signed*) H. RUSSELL WAKEFIELD.

The principal Director of the Methodist Assemblies in America, the Rev. Doctor Davidson, wrote:

"The moral tone of all 'Cheiro' says is uplifting and helpful. I believe in 'Cheiro' and am so far turned from my scepticism that I am going to study further along these lines of thought."

(*Signed*) WILBUR L. DAVIDSON.

The Rev. Minot J. Savage, one of the principals in the Presbyterian Church of Boston, U.S.A., wrote:

"I am greatly interested in the reading of my hand. Its accuracy gives me great respect for the work of 'Cheiro.'"

(*Signed*) M. J. SAVAGE.

I could quote hundreds of other similar testimonies, but "the Church" itself will always remain hostile to the encouragement of any occult studies, forgetting as it does, that all religion is in itself an occult mystery.

In the translation of the Bible from the original Hebrew, any text referring to both Astrology or Palmistry has been altered to suit the religious views held by the translators, a remarkable example of this being the original Hebrew of the 37th chapter of Job and 7th verse, which should read:

"*God placed signs on the hands of men, that all men might know their works.*"

This verse created prolonged discussions during the sixteenth century among theologians, but the interpretation given above was supported by such great minds as Francescus, Schultens, Lyrannus, Thomassin and Debrio.

Opposition from "the Church," dear Reader, you will have to put up with. You will, however, have your revenge when you look round at a Church Bazaar and see the numerous booths presided over by those who practise "the sacred art of Palmistry," and you may have further satisfaction in hearing the announcement that the "disciples of the hand" turned over more money to the Church charity than any of the other attractions.

We will now turn for a moment to the scientific side of the question; why the shape of the hands denote character, and how the lines on the hand are like an open book to those who know how to read them.

First, as regards the shape of the hands: Let us bear in mind, dear Reader, that to a judge of horses the shape and contour of the limbs and especially the hoofs is to such an expert a language in itself.

With one glance such a man will be able to tell you the class and breed the horse represents, he will indicate the kind of work the animal is fit for, and he will even be able to *predict the horse's future*, especially where its career is concerned.

If all this can be done by a person who is a judge of horses by simply looking at the limbs of an animal, how much more so will a person who has made a study of the shape of hands be able to tell all kinds of interesting details from simply looking at the formation of the hand!

If a horse has a clumsy-looking hoof, the animal will also be clumsy, heavy and plodding and not so intelligent as the horse with a refined elegant shaped hoof.

The same rule applies to human beings. A thick-set, clumsy-looking hand will belong to an individual in the lowest scale of intelligence, whereas a long refined-looking type of hand must naturally belong to a superior grade of the human species.

Sir Charles Bell said: "We ought to define the hand as belonging exclusively to man, *corresponding in its sensibility and motion to the endowment of his mind.*"

Quintilian, in writing about what a wonderful thing the hand is, said: "The other parts of the body assist the speaker, but these, I may say, speak for themselves, they ask, they promise, they invoke, they dismiss, they threaten, they entreat, they deprecate, they express fear, joy, grief, our doubts, our assents, our penitence."

We will now see what foundation we get from Science for our belief that the lines on the palm have got a *still greater meaning*.

It is very likely that you have not heard before that there are more sensitory nerves from the brain to the hand than in any other part of the body. These nerves, it stands to reason, by long generations of use, have become so highly developed that the hand, whether passive or active, is in every sense *the willing and obedient servant of every thought that passes in the brain.*

It was the famous Professor Meissner who discovered about 1853 that the corpuscles in the tips of the fingers *and in the lines of the palm* contained the end of the important nerve fibre from the brain, and that during the life of the body *they gave forth certain crepitations or vibrations,* which ceased the moment life became extinct.

Some years later, experiments were carried out in Paris to prove that people with acute hearing could detect the difference in these vibrations in different human beings. In the case of a man who was born blind, but to whom Nature had given an acute sense of hearing, he was able by listening to these vibrations, "to detect the sex, age, temperament, the state of health and *even the subject's nearness to illness and death.*"

This being so, you will now understand why it is that if you searched millions of hands *you will never find* the lines on the hands of any two persons *in this world alike.*

Sir Thomas Browne, in his famous work, "Religio Medici," after referring to Physiognomy, says:

> "Now there are besides these characters in our faces, certain mystical figures in our hands which I dare not call mere dashes, strokes à la volée or at random, because delineated by a pencil that *never works in vain*, and hereof I take more particular notice because I carry that in mine own hand that which I could never read nor discover in another."

As in the study of mankind there came to be recognised a natural position on the face for the nose, or for the eyes, or for the ears, so in this study of the hand there came to be recognised a natural position for the Line of Head, the Line of Life and so on.

Now if you were to meet a man with his nose growing, say, out of his forehead instead of where you know is the natural position, would you not think at once, "What an unnatural man this must be"? and you would be quite right about him.

Follow up the same argument and suppose you were looking at a man or woman's hand and you found the Line of Head shooting upwards towards the base of the fingers instead of being in its natural position across the hand; you would be perfectly right in also saying, "This must be a most unnatural person." You would again be perfectly right in your judgment; but, and this is the wonderful part that I must now call your attention to, you could from the hand, go a step even further. You could say with perfect certainty: "This person is possessed with murderous tendencies," and if you knew the study a little deeper you could go further and say: "At such and such a date in this man's or woman's life he or she *will commit murder.*"

Following the same trend of reasoning, the same study that can show you so accurately the tendency for murder can also show you with equal accuracy the "tendency for success," for after all is said and done—the success of one individual and the non-success of perhaps his brother, is due *to a combination of qualities in each individual.*

If the child born in the most humble cottage in the land has what is called the Line of Success marked clearly in its hand, that child will achieve success in the world *in spite of all obstacles and difficulties.* The lack of training and cultivation will be made up for, the lack of education in the early days will be equalised by harder work in the "night school" of later years, and so on, until the character, will-power, and ability already inherited by the child will force that boy or girl into the "battle of life" and finally *place them in that position that their qualities intend them to have.*

As "the murderer's" tendencies are shown on the hand at the earliest moments of life, so also are the tendencies and qualities that bring success.

This brings us to the point where this study can be of inestimable service to parents and guardians of children, and as well to all men and women who desire to make the most out of their lives.

If you found yourself walking down a road, dear Reader, and you saw in the distance a broken bridge across an abyss, would you not either change your route or wait till the bridge was repaired, or would you take no warning, but go heedlessly on to destruction?

No! I feel sure that you, as an intelligent man or woman, would not do the latter.

By the Study of the Hand you can learn what your tendencies are in advance. You can see whether there is *a break in the road you are on,* or not.

If there is, and you take the warning in time, you can either alter those tendencies that are breaking down "your road" or you may make a new "road" altogether.

That poor man with the "mark of murder" in his hand may as a child have said his prayers nightly at his mother's knees, and yet forget to curb that temper and those passions *that were even then* undermining his will. And that poor mother who in later years heard the death sentence—that the child she loved so much, was "to swing by the rope till dead," how little she thought when those baby hands were clasped nightly in prayer, they had even then a message for her—*a warning of the broken road.*

The agony of it: *not to have known*—the stupidity of it: to have learned all those other things in life and not that one study of the hand *that could have warned her while yet there was time.*

Some people call this study irreligious—some say it is "flying in the face of Providence" to attempt to know the future.

Oh, Religion! How many crimes are done in thy name? How many wrecked lives are piled under thine altars?

The God of Knowledge *rewards knowledge.* He has no patience *with ignorance.* If you put your hand in the fire, it will be burned and *you will suffer* God will not prevent either one or the other—it is knowledge alone that is your protection.

"To know" is the divine right of man. It is

desire for knowledge that makes man superior to the animals.

I therefore hold that the man, or woman, who studies his hand with the desire to know what are his tendencies *is obeying the highest instinct of creation.*

In the same way the young girl who seeks by any study whatever, to find out what are her chances for a happy marriage, is obeying *the most natural mandate of nature.*

If this study should tell her that by waiting a few years longer her chances of happiness would be increased, such a woman has acted with that selfsame prudence and caution that is extolled in the most ordinary affairs of life, and instead of being considered foolish she should be rewarded. *And she will be rewarded,* provided she has acquired the knowledge in order *to make the best of herself.*

That the tendencies that produce deeds and actions in the future are indicated by the lines on our hands *there is no question.* That these tendencies can be changed and so actions in the future altered there is also no question provided that *the effort to change be made long enough in advance.*

This is so seldom done, that Fate sits on the Throne of the Universe and mocks at our blindness.

In thousands of cases I have warned people of "the broken road" and where it led to. As a rule they have laughed at the warning and then railed at God when the payment *had to be made.*

But believe me, dear Reader, the Creator of all things has left no loopholes in His design. All tends towards the ultimate perfection of His plan, which is the highest perfection of mankind, and if that plan is made manifest in the lines and markings of the hand the pursuit of such a study, if carried out in the right spirit for the improvement of self and in consequence the furtherance of the Divine Design, must be one that should appeal to the best instincts of those who take up this study for themselves.

"CHEIRO."

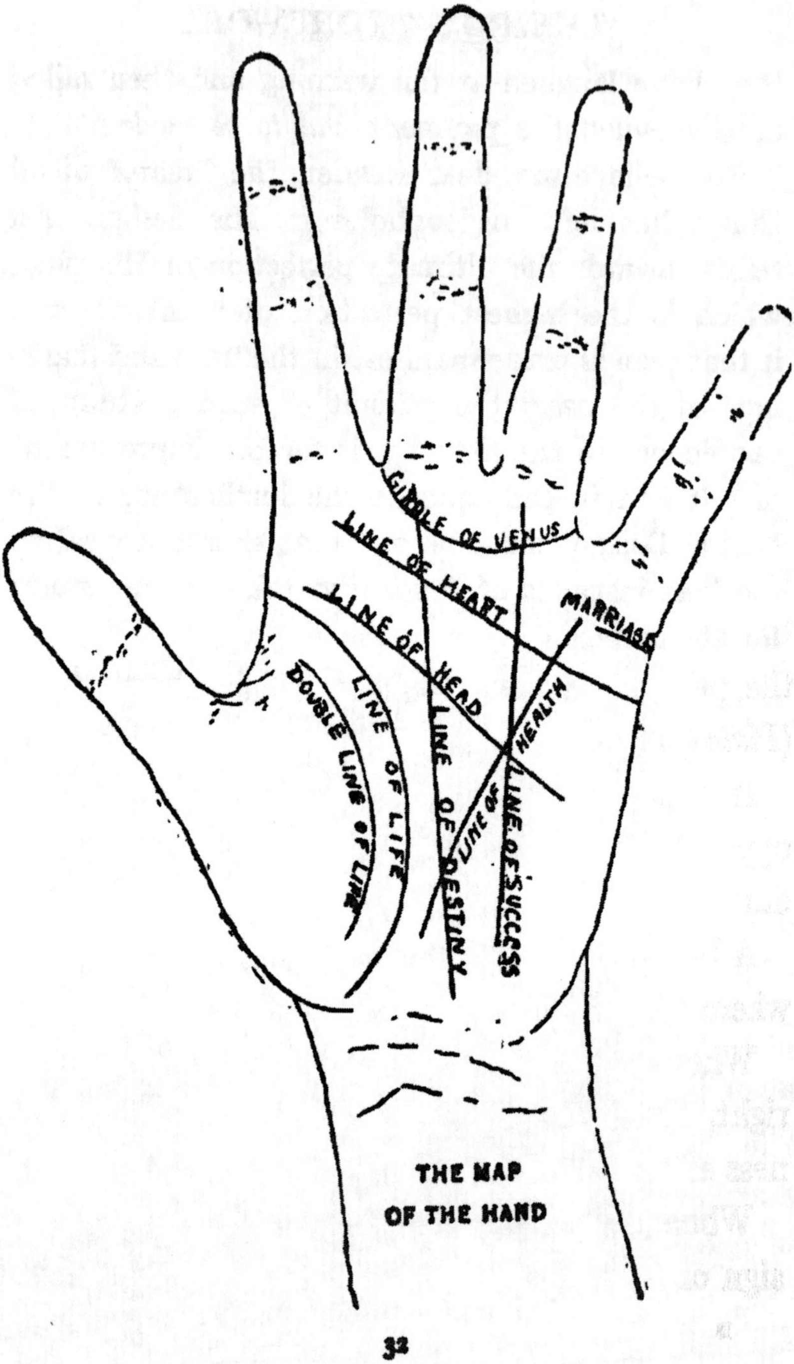

THE MAP OF THE HAND

CHAPTER I

THE LINE OF LIFE

THE Line of Life encircles the ball of the thumb. A short Line of Life is the indication of a short life. A long Line of Life going round the ball of the thumb promises a long life when clear and well marked. (*Plate* 1.)

Lines passing from the Line of Life towards the opposite side of the palm promise long travels and voyages (see dotted lines), but if the main line continues deeply marked round the ball of the thumb the person will always return to his own country. (*Plate* 1.)

If the Line of Life itself bends outwards to the opposite side of the palm, the person will end his days in a far-off land.

A broken Line of Life indicates death at the date where the break is shown. (*Plate* 2.)

When broken in the left hand but joined up in the right, it tells of escape from some dangerous illness and likely death.

When found broken in both hands, it is a certain sign of death.

A double Line of Life (see inner line) which is also called the Line of Mars, indicates great vitality. (*Plate 2.*) If found passing behind the broken Line of Life it promises that the life will continue no matter how serious the illness or accident may be.

When this Line of Mars sends an offshoot through the Line of Life to the opposite side of the hand (see dotted line) it foretells rashness and heed-

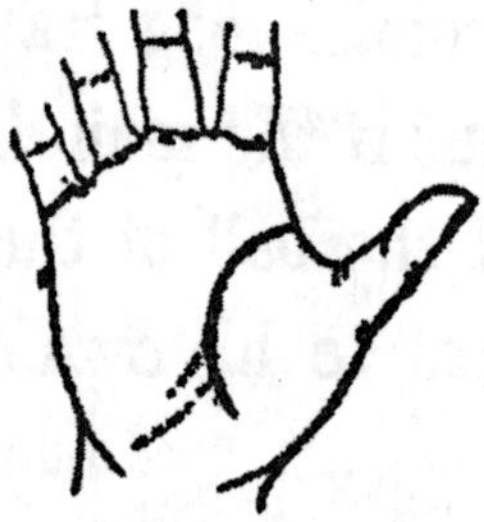

The Line of Life
Plate 1

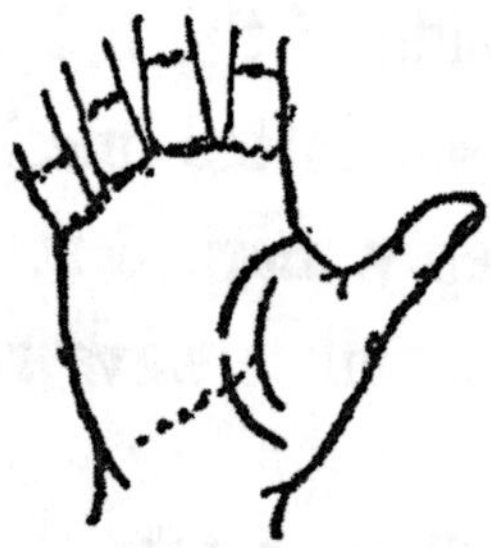

The Line of Life
Plate 2

lessness of danger which will in itself threaten death at the point where it cuts through the Line of Life. (*Plate 2.*)

When the Line of Life is linked like a chain or made up of little pieces it is a sure sign of delicacy and ill-health. If the chain formation is followed by a clear, well-marked line, then the health will recover at the date where the line becomes clear. But if the chain or little pieces continue all through the Line of

Life bad health will persist until the end. (*Plate* 3.)

If many fine lines are seen with such a Line of Life, passing through it from the Line of Mars towards the opposite base of the palm, the ill-health will be largely brought about by the person craving for excitement, intemperance and such like causes (see dotted lines). (*Plate* 3.)

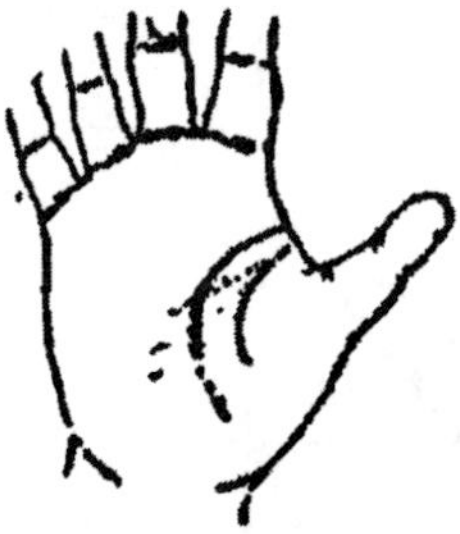

The Line of Life
Plate 3

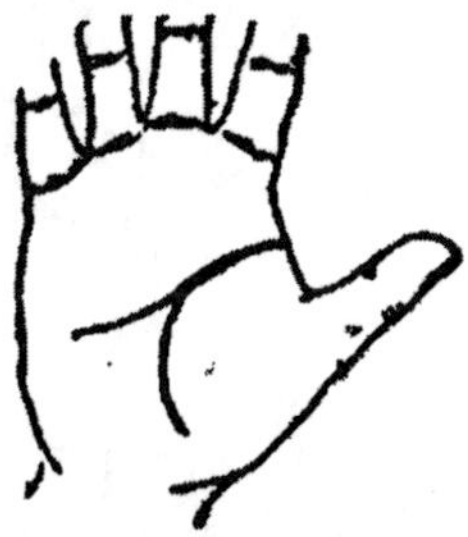

The Line of Life
Plate 4

When the Line of Life and the Line of Head are seen as it were *clinging together* half-way down the palm, it is a sign of a highly nervous, over-sensitive person. With a thin or weak-looking Life Line, such an individual would worry himself into bad health. He is also over-timid, over cautious and has little courage in facing the realities of life. (*Plate* 4.)

When, on the contrary, the Line of Life and that of Head are only slightly connected together the person will be both sensitive and cautious, but not unduly so.

When the Line of Life has the appearance of lying closely in to the ball of the thumb (also called the Mount of Venus) and so making this part of the palm look narrow, the physical or vital forces are

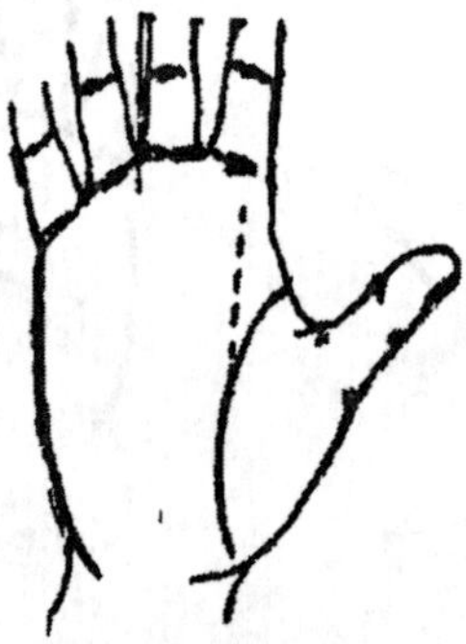

The Line of Life
Plate 5

never robust. (*Plate* 5.) Such persons have little or no passion in their love affairs and if married are generally sterile and seldom have children.

The contrary is the case when the Line of Life sweeps out into the palm and makes the ball of the thumb large and prominent.

CHAPTER II

THE LINE OF HEAD

THE Line of Head, otherwise called the Line of Mentality, lying straight across the palm, indicates a "level-headed" person and in this position promises success in business and all practical matters. (*Plate* 1.)

When sloping downwards towards the wrist or towards the opposite base of the palm, it denotes imagination, invention, romance, ideality and the artistic qualities. (*Plate* 2.)

When still more sloping and especially when formed slightly curving as it were under the Mount on the base of the opposite side of the palm, excess of imagination, extreme sensitiveness, melancholy and a tendency towards suicide. (*Plate* 3.)

When turning upwards towards the "little finger" it denotes a violent nature, danger of murder for personal greed or gain, an intensely determined, self-willed disposition. (*Plate* 4.)

The Line of Head when separated from the Line of Life, indicates self-confidence, impulsiveness, quickness, but inclined to rashness and foolhardiness when the space is very wide. (*Plate* 5.)

When *closely joined* to the Line of Life, it denotes lack of self-confidence, great caution and extreme sensitiveness. (*Plate* 6.)

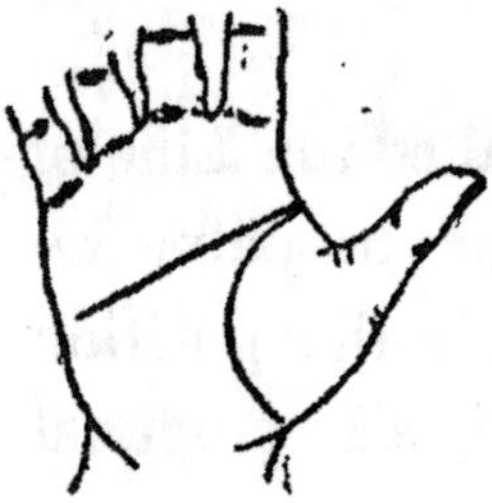

The Line of Head
Plate 1

The Line of Head
Plate 2

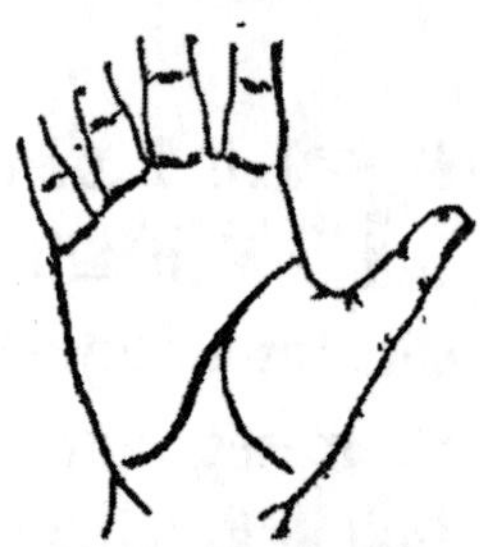

The Line of Head
Plate 3

The Line of Head
Plate 4

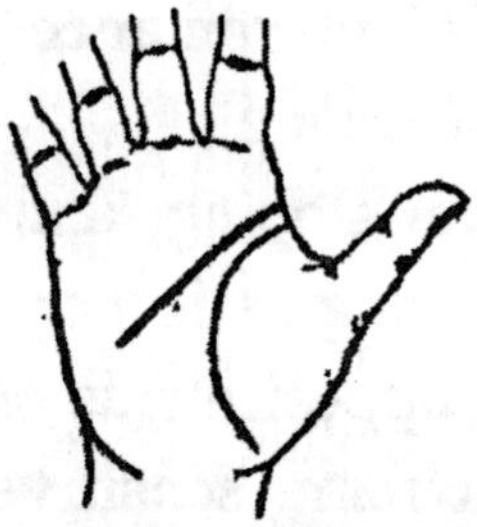

The Line of Head
Plate 5

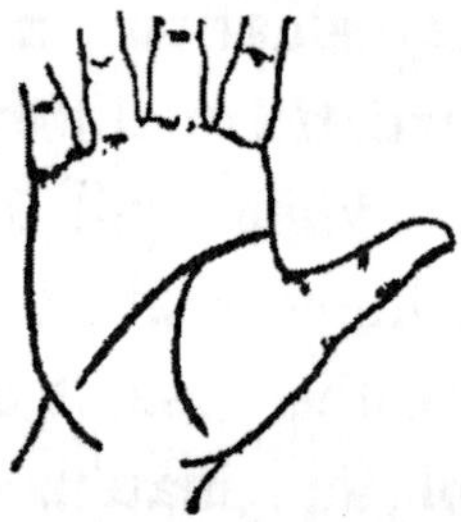

The Line of Head
Plate 6

When found as one straight line across the palm from side to side, it denotes unusual brain power of the practical order, but the person is likely to go to extremes in all he attempts. If, however, the Line of Heart (under the base of the fingers) is found at the same time on such a hand, it modifies these qualities, and prevents the person from being as hard or as self-contained as the Line of Head across the palm would by itself denote. (*Plate* 7.)

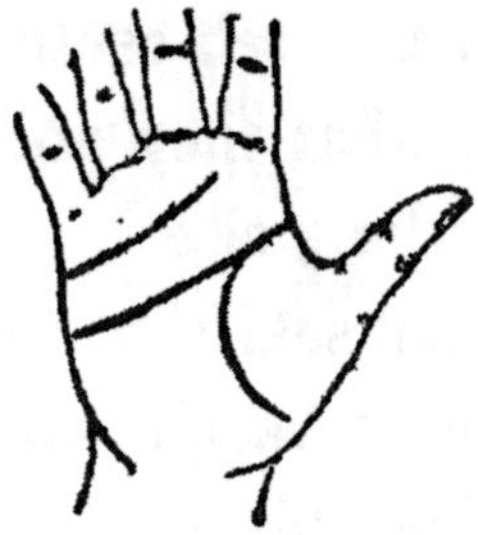

The Line of Head
Plate 7

When the Lines of Head and Heart appear to be joined together and run in one straight mark across the palm from side to side, the person will be as equally determined in his love affairs as he will be in all other matters on which he sets his mind. (*Plate* 8.)

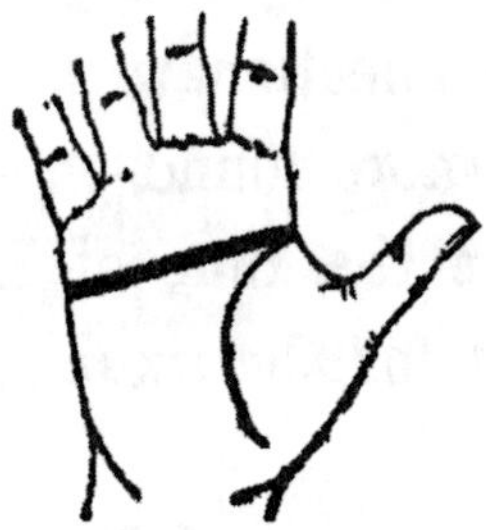

The Line of Head
Plate 8

If they love, they do so with all the intensity of their nature; if they hate or dislike, they are equally intense. Such persons will wait for years for the one they love; in their hate they will equally wait for their revenge.

They are extremely "self-centred," generally very "wrapped up" in what they are engaged in to the exclusion of everything else.

This is a very unusual sign to have and is only found in about *one to ten thousand.* For this reason a person possessing this mark has *few real companions.* If other signs in the hand are good, such as the Line of Fate or Line of Success, the possessors of this curious sign may expect in the end to realise their ambitions, whether it be in love or in material matters.

This sign must not be confused with what is known as "the Murderer's mark," where the Line of Head *turns upward* or runs *through or against* the Line of Heart, and by doing so appears to crush or annihilate the affectionate nature. The "Murderer's mark" is more found on a coarse thick-set short hand, where the Line of Head *rises against* the Line of Heart (or the more human side of the nature).

When the main Lines of Head, Heart and Life are joined together, as in (*Plate* 9), it denotes danger of accidents and a violent death, but one brought on *by some peculiarity in the person's own disposition.* These individuals never seem to be able

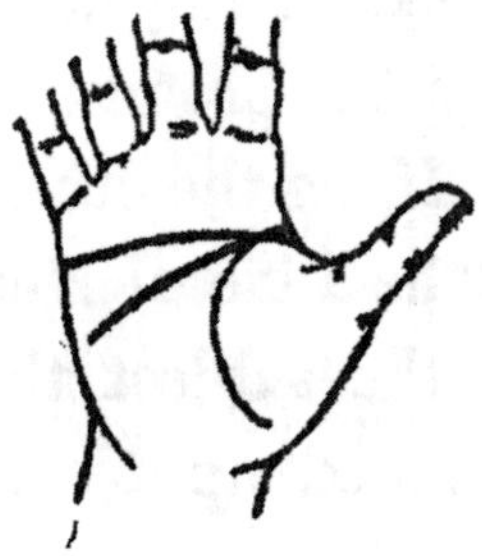

The Line of Head
Plate 9

to avoid danger—they appear to run into it or attract it, as for example, in a critical moment they appear to "lose their head" and do the wrong thing.

MORE DETAILS ABOUT THE LINE OF HEAD AND ITS MEANINGS

In my work I regard the Line of Head, or the Line of Mentality, as the most important sign that can be found in the hand. A Line of Head is like the needle in the compass, without a true knowledge of which it is impossible to grasp the "direction of the subject." I have seen more mistakes caused by a lack of grasp of this point than by anything else.

I have known, for example, many students make the mistake of paying great attention to what looked like a good Line of Success, and, at the same time, not noticing a weak, badly-formed Line of Head, which contradicted the promise of success given by the various lines. If, on the other hand, the student had first noticed the Line of Head, he would have been able to tell the subject that the promise of success was not backed up by the intelligence or the mentality.

As regards the future being foreshadowed, it has been demonstrated that the brain is always growing, changing, increasing or diminishing. These changes commence *years before the effect is shown by the thoughts or actions of the individual*. A boy ten years old may at that point commence a development which will not be felt until he is thirty, and then it may change his whole life and career. As this development commences at ten, even at that age it has affected certain nerves, and they in their turn *have already affected the Line of Head—a full twenty years before the point of change or action has been reached.* It therefore follows that the future may be seen and told by a careful examination of the hand which, as Aristotle has said, is the "organ of all organs, the active agent of the passive powers of the entire system."

The Line of Head, or indication of the Mentality of the subject, must in all cases be considered as the most important line on the hand. The greatest attention should be paid to it, so as to obtain a clear grasp of the Mentality under consideration.

The two hands must be carefully compared—the left showing *the inherited tendencies*,—the right the *developed or cultivated qualities*. The slightest change or deviation in the markings from the left to the right should be carefully noted down or remembered.

The direction or the termination or end of the line should, above all, be distinctly noted, for the all-important reason that this shows the direction that the Mentality *is inclined to develop towards*. For example, if found with the end of the line sloping downwards in the left hand, and straight across the palm in the right, the student is safe in concluding that the subject has not been able to follow his natural bent, but by the force of circumstances has been obliged to make himself more practical, to study business methods, and to have undertaken a training towards practicality and level-headedness in order to rise equal to the circumstances that he found himself forced to meet.

In this way the student obtains an insight into the earlier conditions of the life under examination that is invaluable, especially when there is, as will be found in many cases, no Line of Destiny visible in the early years.

The Line of Head may commence in three distinct ways, namely:

From inside the Line of Life.
Joined to the Line of Life.
Outside the Line of Life.

Its general characteristics are as follows:

When straight, clear and even, it denotes practical common sense and business capability.

When sloping—a leaning for romance, ideality, the artistic, and all imaginative qualities.

When straight, clear, and going well out across the palm, the subject has great intellectual power, would be long-headed and extremely practical.

When straight and curving slightly at the end upwards towards the "little finger" the subject would make a great success in a business life, but would be grasping and hard over money matters.

CHAPTER III

THE LINE OF HEART

THE Line of Heart is found at the base of the Mounts under the fingers. It denotes the Love nature and relates to all matters dealing with the affections. (*Plate* 1.)

When appearing more pronounced and more heavily marked than the Line of Head, the desire

The Line of Heart
Plate 1

The Line of Heart
Plate 2

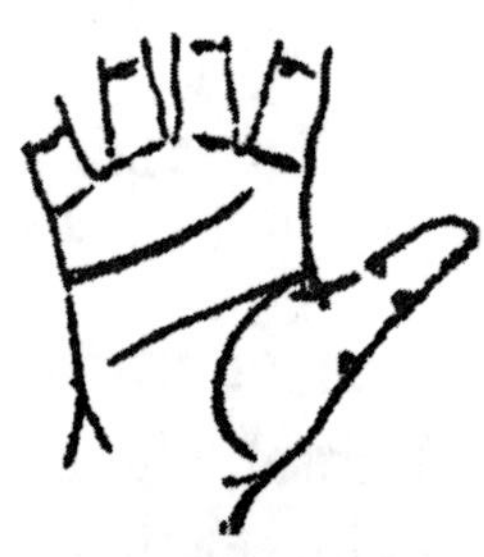

The Line of Heart
Plate 3

for Love and Affection will outweigh all other interests. (*Plate* 2.)

When the Line of Heart is very pronounced but with a good Line of Head, the Love nature will be employed for the good of others. (*Plate* 3.)

When the Line of Heart begins *under the first finger*, the man or woman will dictate and "lay down the law" in all matters of the Affections. (*Plate* 4.)

Starting from under the base of the *second finger* the Line of Heart denotes a more placid Love nature—a woman who puts the accent on the word OBEY in the Marriage Service. (*Plate* 5.)

When the Line of Heart is deeply marked with a number of small lines running into it and with a

The Line of Heart
Plate 4

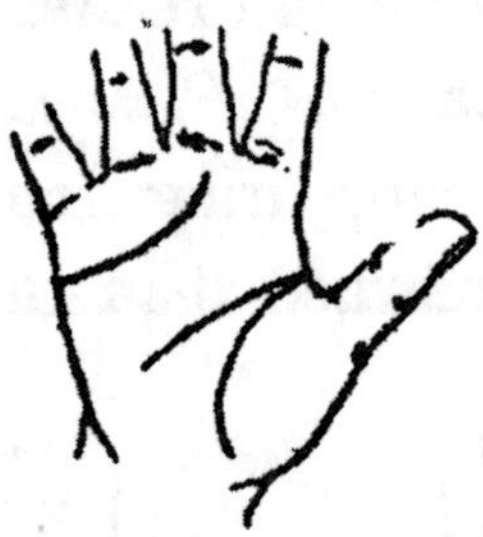

The Line of Heart
Plate 5

large or pronounced Mount of Venus (base of the thumb), the emotional, passionate nature will dominate the life. Famous dramatic singers and emotional actresses always have these indications. (*Plate* 6.)

When the Line of Heart is not as pronounced as is the Line of Head, the Love nature is over mastered by the mental desires. Such persons put Love on one side, they generally lead lonely or rather isolated lives, they rarely, if ever, marry, but if they do they become more mental companions than wives or husbands in the true sense of the expression. (*Plate* 7.)

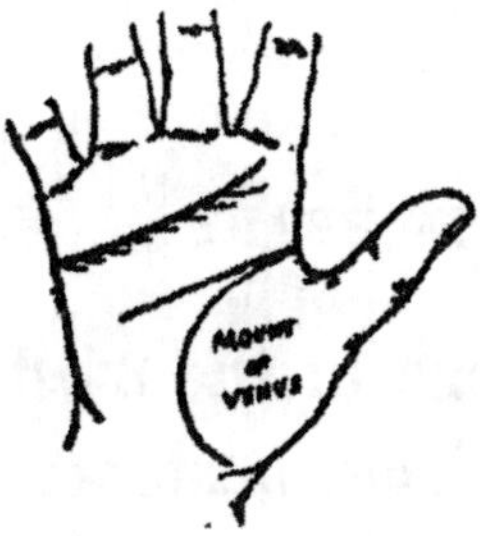

The Line of Heart
Plate 6

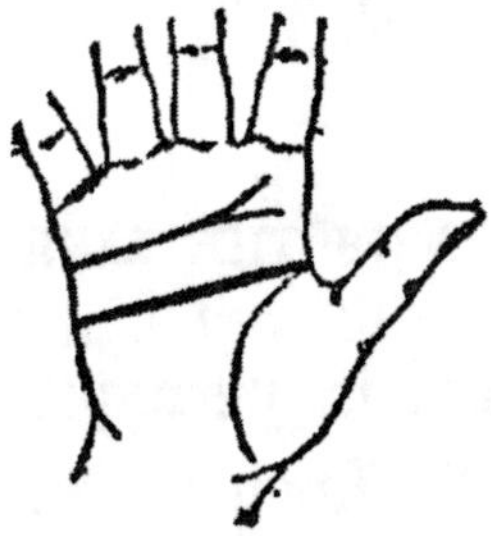

The Line of Heart
Plate 7

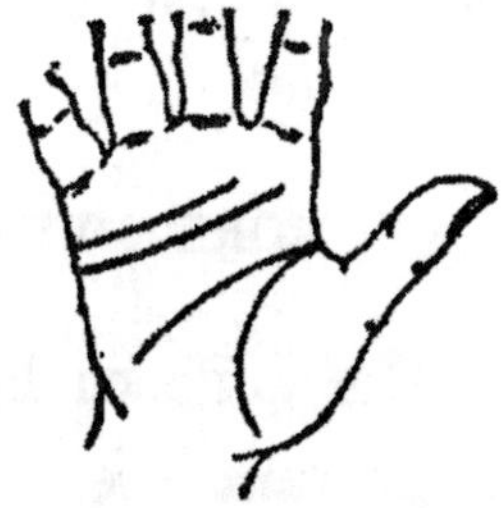

The Line of Heart
Plate 8

A "double Line of Heart" denotes the Love nature in excess, but if the Line of Head is long and sloping, the Love nature devotes itself to the good of others. Such persons sacrifice themselves to carry

The Line of Heart
Plate 9

out wonderful plans for the uplifting and redemption of humanity. (*Plate* 8.)

When the Line of Heart appears to be opposed or controlled by the Line of Head rising upwards against it, the Affections are suppressed or crushed by the desires of the brain. Such persons sacrifice *all* to their *love of money* and will stick at nothing to obtain it. (*Plate* 9.)

MORE DETAILS OF THE LINE OF HEART

The Line of Heart is, perhaps, one of the most important lines of all. Love, under all circumstances and in all ages, has played the leading rôle in the drama of life, and, as in nature, so in the hand.

The Line of Heart may rise from the middle of the Mount under the first finger, between the first and second fingers, and also from the middle of the Mount under the second finger.

Rising under the first finger, we get the highest type of love—the worship of the ideal. A man or woman with such a formation would be an enthusiast, they would pour out their hearts in homage to the person they love. At the same time they would demand love in return, they would dictate and "lay down the law" as to how they should be loved.

Such natures, I need hardly add, are somewhat difficult to live with.

The Line of Heart rising between the first and second finger, the subjects have a quieter nature in matters of love. They seem to rest between the ideality given by first type and the tendency to materialism given by the third class. They are quieter and more subdued in their passions; they are capable of deep affection, but they regard love more in a calm and tranquil way.

When the Line of Heart rises from under the second finger, the subjects have an even quieter, almost fatalist devotion, and, as a rule, are more or less 'self-contained in their affection. They have great control over their feelings, and are not so expressive or demonstrative as those with the line from under the base of the first finger.

When the Line of Heart goes right across the hand from side to side, an excess of affection is the result, and a great tendency to jealousy.

When the Line of Heart is chained and fretted by a crowd of little lines, it tells of inconstancy, inveterate flirtations, a series of amourettes, but no lasting affection.

A Line of Heart with the chain formation from under the second finger gives an utter contempt for the opposite sex.

When the Line of Heart is bright red, it denotes great violence of passion.

When pale and broad, the nature is blasé and indifferent.

Lying low down, close to the Line of Head and when the latter is deeply marked, the affections are completely controlled by the brain; such people are usually cold and calculating.

A person with no Line of Heart is hard, cold, devoid of affection, and generally possessed of an iron, unbending will.

Breaks in the Line of Heart tell of disappointment and trouble—under the second finger, fatality; under the third finger, by pride; and under the fourth, by folly or avarice.

When the Line of Heart is forked on the base of the first finger, it is an unfailing sign of trueness of heart, and enthusiasm in love.

When the line forks with one branch under the second finger, the other running between the first and second fingers, it is a sign of good fortune in matters of affection, but of a tranquil nature.

A Line of Heart, bare and thin, towards the percussion, or side of the hand, denotes sterility and a cold reserved nature.

When the line is quite bare of branches, it tells of coldness of heart and want of affection.

Fine lines rising up to the Line of Heart from the palm tell of those who affect our lives, and, by being crossed or uncrossed denote if the affection has brought trouble or otherwise.

CHAPTER IV

THE LINE OF FATE OR DESTINY

THE Line of Fate or Destiny is the line from the wrist to the second finger. When long and well marked it denotes strong personality and if the other lines on the hand are good it promises success by one's own personal individuality. (*Plate* I.)

If found turning towards the base of the first finger, or sending a branch towards it (see dotted line), it promises that the person will have a position of rule and authority over others. (*Plate* I.)

If bending towards, or sending a branch to the third finger (see dotted line), it foretells fame, glory, and public life; but more that of the sensational kind as in the case of actors, barristers, great orators or those in the "public eye," whereas when going to the base of the first finger it gives more the position of responsibility and rule over others, such as in the case of great statesmen, kings, presidents, princes, governors, generals, or in a lesser degree, heads of business and successful employers and controllers of men. (*Plate* I.)

When "broken" it foretells trouble and disaster at whatever date the "break" appears. (*Plate* 2.) The centre of the palm is considered the middle of the Destiny or thirty-five years of age.

In a later chapter the system of how exact dates are found will be given in detail.

The Line of Fate when it appears joined or tied to the Line of Life, indicates sacrifice to others during the early part of the career. This is generally

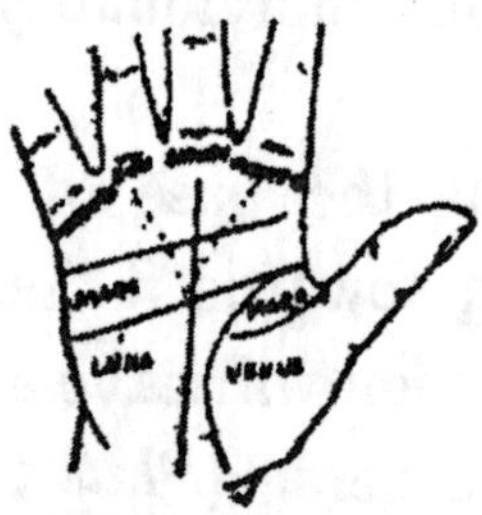

The Line of Fate
Plate 1

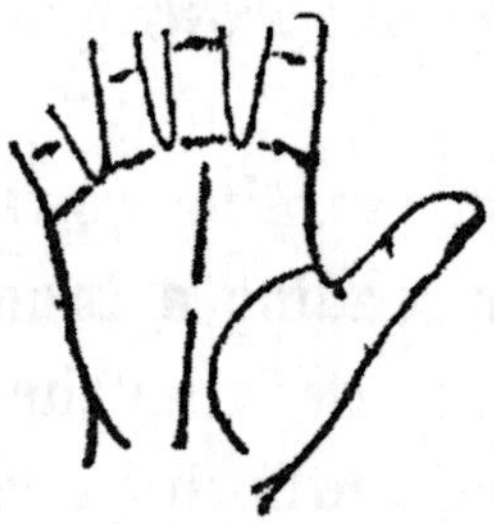

The Line of Fate
Plate 2

found on the hands of men or women who have put aside their own ambitions in order to support their parents or other relations; it is also often seen in the case of early marriages, where the Fate has been hampered by the cares and responsibilities of family ties. (*Plate* 3.)

The Line of Fate starting from *inside* the Line of Life or from any part on the base of the Thumb (also called the Mount of Venus) denotes that the Love nature—or on a hand with a weak

Line of Head, the sensual disposition—rules and cripples the career. (*Plate* 4.)

The Line of Fate starting from the centre or from the opposite side of the palm shows a destiny independent of home ties or other influences from the commencement. This also gives an insight into the character and shows that the person will not readily sacrifice themselves for others; with a very

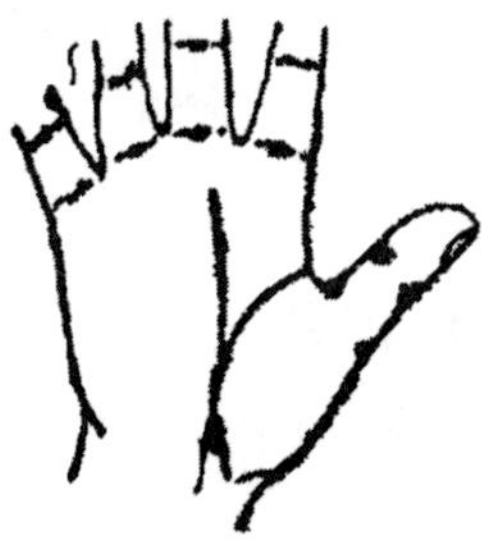

The Line of Fate
Plate 3

The Line of Fate
Plate 4

The Line of Fate
Plate 5

straight Line of Head this is invariably the case. (*Plate* 5.)

The farther out the Line of Fate commences near the outside of the base of the palm, the less the person is influenced by "home ties" or even the wishes of other people.

When no Line of Fate is found on the hand, there will be a hard struggle for existence all through the life.

When an "island" is formed on the Line of Fate, it is not as bad a sign as the "break," but it indicates trouble and loss of power or position as long as the "island" lasts. (*Plate* 6.)

When the Line of Fate separates, and one line commences before the other ends, it is not the indication of "a broken fate," but means a *complete change in the career*. If the line appears to continue stronger in appearance after this mark, then the change will be to the advantage of the person

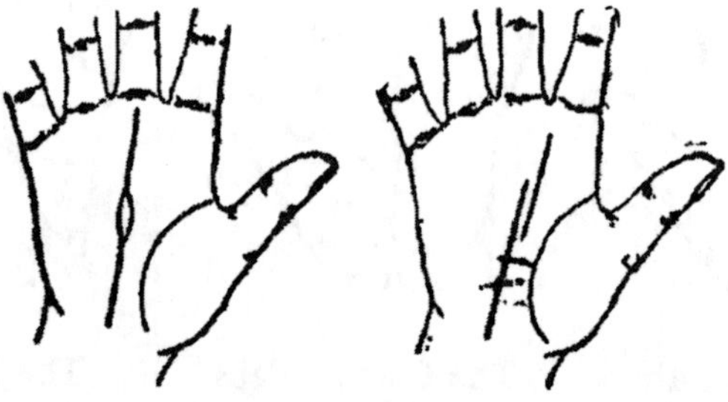

The Line of Fate *Plate* 6 — The Line of Fate *Plate* 7

on whose hand it is shown. The reverse is the case when the continuing line looks weaker or fades out altogether. (*Plate* 7.)

From this it will be seen how changes in the career (whether for good luck or the reverse) may be seen years in advance and might be altered one way or the other if the warning is acted upon in time.

The Line of Fate is like the railway of Destiny—it has its junctions, its sidings, its broken bridges. If the driver of an engine paid no regard to his signals, the broken bridge would not be repaired in time, or the siding he might be running into may lead to nowhere.

FURTHER INDICATIONS OF THE LINE OF FATE OR DESTINY

The Line of Fate or Destiny relates to our worldly advancement, and to our position and success.

It may rise from the Line of Life, the wrist, the outside base of the palm, or from the middle of the palm.

Rising from the Line of Life, success will be won by personal merit, but if the line be tied down by the Line of Life, the early portion of the subject's life will be sacrificed to the wishes of parents, relatives, by early burdens, and duties to one's family.

When the line rises from the wrist and goes straight up the hand, it is a sign of extreme good fortune, luck, and denotes a strong personality.

Rising from the outside of the palm, the person is of a very independent nature—but has more the travelling, roving spirit of adventure than when the line rises up the centre of the hand. If such a line joins the Line of Heart and continues with it to the first finger, it foretells prosperity through the affections, but brought about by romance and chance.

If the Line of Fate be straight and a line runs in and joins it from the outside of the palm, it tells that some person will assist and back up the subject in his pursuit of fame, ambition and worldly success.

If the line goes on to the base of the second finger, but sends offshoots on to the other mounts, it denotes that science, commerce, or art will change the life according to whatever mount indicated.

If the line itself, or any branch of it, should go to any mount or portion of the hand instead of to the second finger, it foretells great success in that particular direction.

Going to the Mount of Mercury (see *Plate* 1)—distinction in science, eloquence or commerce.

To the Mount of the Sun (see *Plate* 1)—distinction in art, literature, dramatic work or public life.

Art, if the third finger be fine and pointed.

Literature, if the third finger be square.

Dramatic work, if the nail phalange of the third finger be spatulate.

If the Line of Fate go up to the Mount of Jupiter (see *Plate* 1) the Fate and work of the subject will be to win ambition and power, to dictate or rule over others.

When the line cuts into the third phalange of the

finger of Saturn, it is not a happy sign, as everything will go too far.

When stopped by the Line of Heart, fortune will be ruined by the affections. When, however, it joins the Line of Heart, and they together ascend the Mount of Jupiter, it is a magnificent sign. The subject will gain high position, and get his highest ambitions gratified through love.

When stopped by the Line of Head, it foretells that fortune will be spoiled through miscalculation, or by stupidity.

If the line does not rise until late in the middle of the palm (the Plain of Mars) it tells of a hard life; but if it goes on well to the second finger, all difficulties will be conquered through the subject's energy and will.

If it only rises from the Line of Head, and that line is good, success will be won late in life through the subject's talent and perseverance.

When the line rises with one branch from Luna, the other from Venus, wild dreams of imagination and love will lead to success or failure, according to the length and strength of the Line of Fate.

When broken and irregular, the Fate will be full of trouble and worry..

A break is not always a bad sign: when one branch begins *before the other leaves off*, it is a sign of a change in life, and of an advancement in position if the line continues strong.

When the line joins it and goes on, either as an attendant or as a short ray line, it is generally marriage, or the influence of some other person over one's life.

A double or sister fate line, I have always proved to be an excellent sign, particularly if it goes up to different mounts.

People with no Line of Fate whatever generally lead a mere vegetable existence. They go through life in a mechanical way. They eat, drink, sleep, and —well, I cannot say—are happy, for they cannot feel acutely, and to feel happiness we must also feel the reverse. Sunshine and shadow, smiles and tears, comprise the sum total of our lives.

CHAPTER V

THE LINE OF SUCCESS, OTHERWISE CALLED THE LINE OF SUN

THE Line of Success or of Sun is as the Sun is to the Earth, whenever it appears on the hand it promises brightness, success, and increase of fortune. Its best position is rising from the wrist to the base of the third finger. (*Plate* 1.)

When this line rises on the inside of the Line of Life (Mount of Venus) riches or success come. through Love such as produced by a wealthy union (*Plate* 2.)

When rising from the extreme outside base of the hand (otherwise known as the Mount of Luna or the Moon) the success promised depends more on the caprice of the public and is usually associated with public favourites, such as stage or film stars, singers, artists who create sensational work, and such-like. (*Plate* 3.) In this position it never promises such solid or lasting fame or glory as if the line rises stright from the wrist or later on from the centre of the palm or from the Line of Fate.

Rising out of, or from the Line of Fate, the Line of Success is more certain in its promise that the career of the person will be successful. From whatever date it leaves the Fate Line it denotes that from that exact time the individual will begin to reap the

The Line of Success
Plate 1

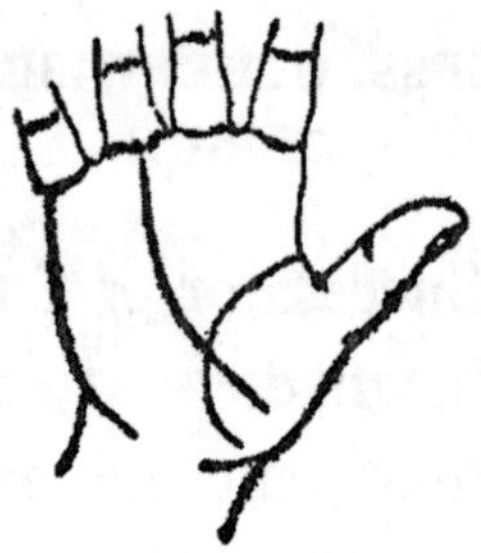

The Line of Success
Plate 2

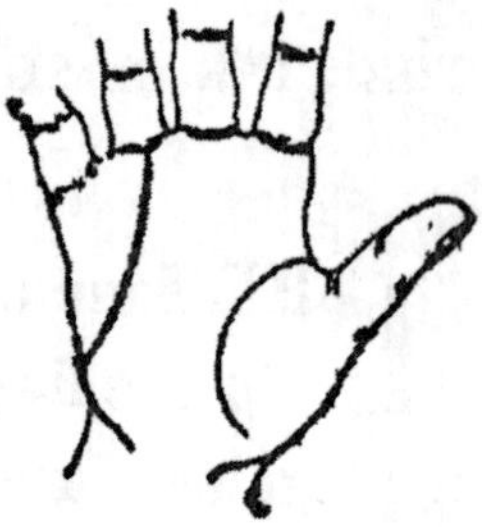

The Line of Success
Plate 3

reward he or she has worked for. (*Plate* 4.) If it continues without any breaks up to the base of the third finger, so will the success be equally continuous.

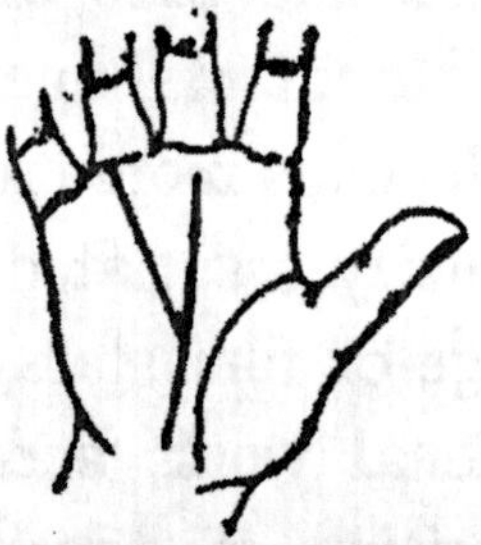

The Line of Success
Plate 4

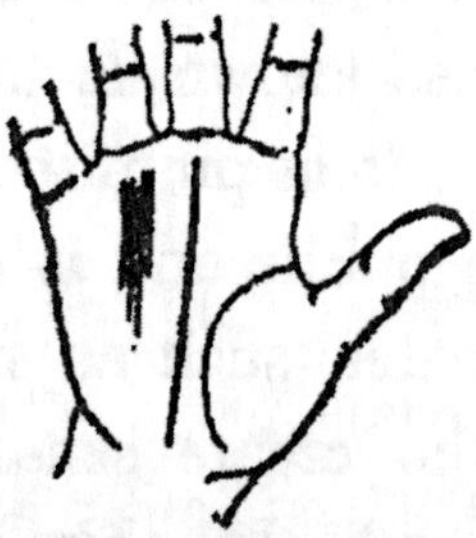

The Line of Success
Plate 5

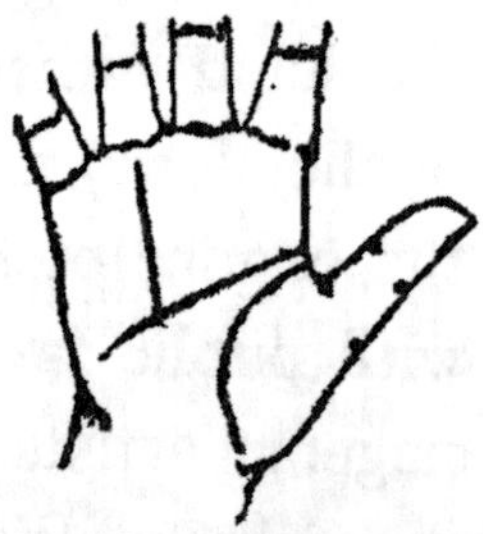

The Line of Success
Plate 6

A number of small lines from the centre of the palm to the third finger are also fortunate, but not so good or as important as one long line equal in strength and appearance to the Line of Fate itself.

A number of lines usually denotes that the person's success will be divided by different aims and ambitions. (*Plate* 5.)

When this line first makes its appearance from the Line of Head, success will begin only after middle life and will come from the person's own mental work; there is no element of what is called "luck" when it is in that position. (*Plate* 6.)

The Line of Success
Plate 7

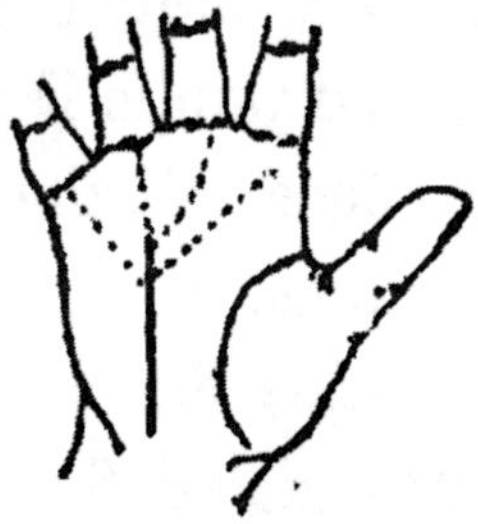

The Line of Success
Plate 8

When the Line of Sun has a gap in it, it is called "broken," and all success and luck will cease while the break lasts.

When it appears with a loop or "island" in it (*Plate* 7), this sign is not as bad as if the line is "broken," but the "island" foretells scandal, notoriety, and damaging publicity at the date the "island" appears (dates and times will be explained in a following chapter).

When the Line of Success sends a branch from it to any other Mount under the base of the fingers, the success promised takes after the qualities of that particular Mount. (*Plate* 8.)

Examples: A branch to the first finger (Mount of Jupiter) promises success and fame in rule and authority over others.

To the base of the second finger (Mount of Saturn or Fate) the man or woman is more the "child of Fate," such as that "man of Destiny," Napoleon.

To its own Mount (The Sun) success, glory, happiness and public life.

To the base of the fourth finger (Mount of Mercury) success in commerce, science and practical matters. (*Plate* 8.)

When no line of Sun or Success is found on a hand, there is no element of "luck" or "chance" in the career. There will be little happiness, brightness or fame, but if the Line of Fate is prominent the person may be equally powerful in whatever his career may be, but he will get little or no credit in a public sense for whatever he may do.

FURTHER DETAILS ON THE LINE OF THE SUN OR SUCCESS

The Line of the Sun is the most favourable sign found on the hand.

It may rise from the Line of Life, the Line of

Head, the Mount of Luna, the centre of the palm, otherwise called the Plain of Mars, or from the Line of Heart.

Rising from the Line of Life, it promises great success won by talent and *personal merit.* If found in a hand without any special development it is even then a sure sign of ultimate success.

From the Mount of Luna, it foretells success and distinction, but largely dependent upon others. In this case it is not a certain sign of success, it being so influenced by the fortunes of others. With a sloping Line of Head, however, it gives success in poetry, literature, the arts, and all original and imaginative work.

Rising from the centre of the palm, the Plain of Mars, it is not nearly so good, success being only won after difficulty, by hard work, personal merit, perseverance, fighting and exertion.

Rising from the Line of Heart, it gives great taste for art and artistic things; but these people never make much use of their artistic life, unless the finger of the Sun be spatulate, then the tendency of life would be for dramatic art, and if the Line of Head be good, these subjects make distinct success in all dramatic work and in public life, but success comes late in life.

If the third finger be nearly equal with the second

finger in length, a Line of Sun with such formation will give a passion for gambling, and often great success in speculation of all kinds.

This line invariably gives a tendency towards sensitiveness, a nature that feels and knows its own worth, and is, consequently, extremely *sensitive to the opinion of the world.*

With a straight Line of Head, the Line of the Sun only gives a love of attaining riches, and of material things.

Many lines on the Mount of the Sun denote an extremely artistic nature, but multiplicity of ideas will interfere with success. Such people always have a craving for reputation, and the desire to be famous but generally attempt too many things at the same time.

A star on this line is, perhaps, the finest sign that can be found. Brilliant success is, with the possessor, a certainty.

On a hollow hand, this line loses all power.

The complete absence of the Line of the Sun on an otherwise long artistic-shaped hand, denotes hard work in any branch of art attempted. These people may deserve success, but they seldom get it. The world generally acknowledges them too late. These are the artists who die in poverty and get monuments only over their graves.

CHAPTER VI

THE LINE OF HEALTH

THE Line of Health begins under the "little finger," and goes down the palm towards the Line of Life. (*Plate* 1.)

When the Line of Life tound the base of the thumb is made up of little pieces or linked like a chain and the Line of Health is thick and heavy,

The Line of Health
Plate 1

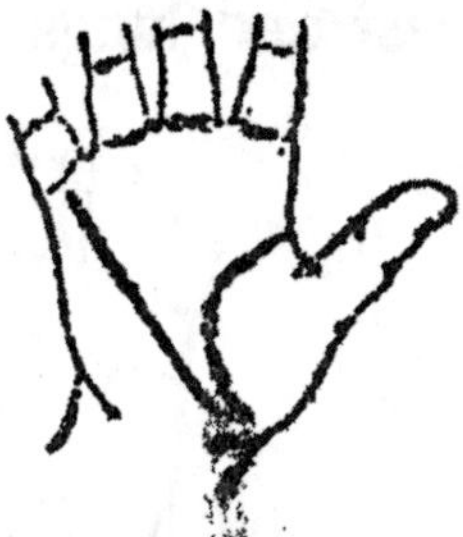

The Line of Health
Plate 2

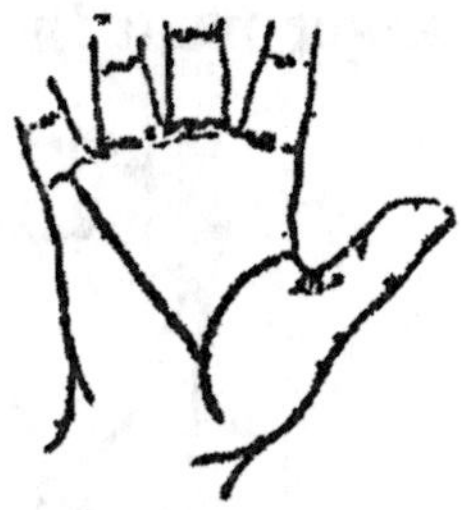

The Line of Health
Plate 3

great delicacy and illness may be expected all through life. (*Plate* 2.)

When the Line of Health or any branch from it touches the Line of Life, it foretells severe illness and danger of death at the date the two lines meet. (*Plate* 3.)

The Line of Health with a loop or "island" in it near but above the Line of Head denotes trouble with nose and throat. (*Plate* 4.)

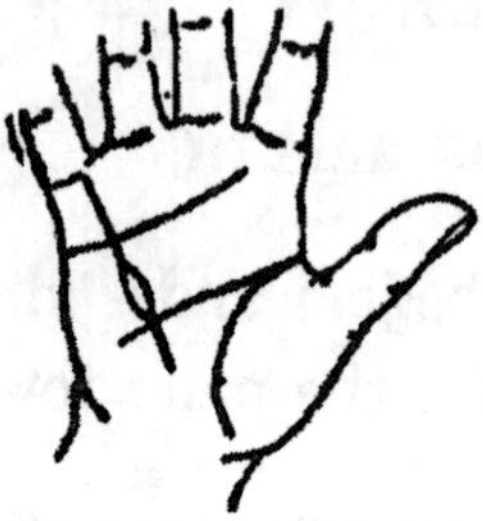

The Line of Health
Plate 4

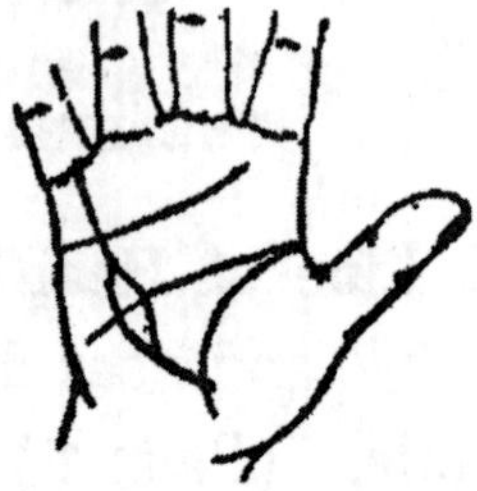

The Line of Health
Plate 5

The Line of Health forming an "island" *above and below* the Line of Head indicates delicacy and danger from the chest and lungs, and especially so

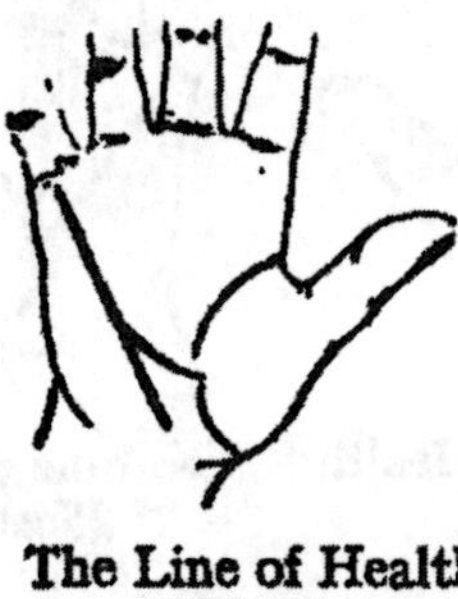

The Line of Health
Plate 6

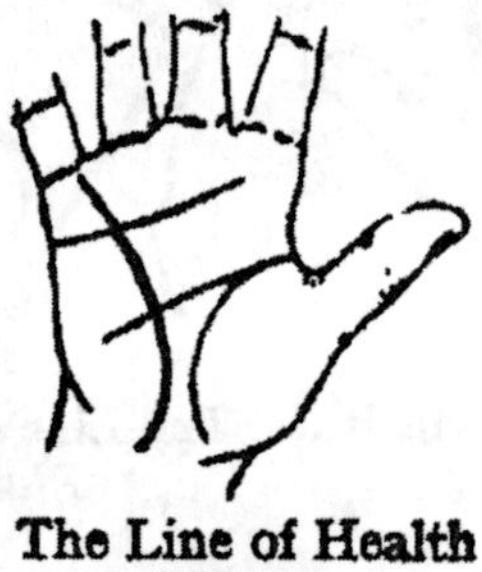

The Line of Health
Plate 7

when the finger nails are long and "almond shape." (*Plate* 5.)

Danger of death is clearly indicated when the Line of Life is "broken" and a branch from the Line of Health or the Line itself runs into the "break." (*Plate* 6.)

When the Line of Health appears to turn away from the Line of Life, it denotes complete recovery from whatever illness threatened, and this sign is in itself the promise of a very long life. (*Plate 7.*)

It is best of all to have *no* Line of Health on the hand.

FURTHER REMARKS ON THE LINE OF HEALTH

This Line of Health rises at the base of the "little finger," and grows down the palm towards the Line of Life. It should not cross over to, or cut, the Line of Life.

The straighter it lies on the hand the better.

Touching the Line of Life, it indicates that there is some delicacy at work undermining the life.

Joining both Lines of Heart and Life together and so forming a narrow triangle on the palm, it denotes a tendency for weakness of the heart, especially if an "island" appears in the Heart Line,

The Line of Health deep and very red in colour denotes a tendency to fevers.

Twisted, irregular and dark in colour—biliousness and liver complaints.

If very heavy when crossing the Line of Head—severe headaches.

When very broken—bad digestion and poor health.

With an "island" above the Line of Head—delicacy of nose and throat.

With a large "island" above and below the Line of Head—delicacy of chest and lungs.

Joining the Lines of Heart and Head together only, it indicates a danger to the brain—very often of fever, especially so if "islands" are marked on the Line of Head.

A long straight Line of Health turning away from the Life Line will counteract the evil effects of a weak Line of Life.

CHAPTER VII

INDICATIONS OF MARRIAGE

THE Line of Marriage is found between the Line of Heart and the base of the fourth finger.

When found straight and clear it promises a happy marriage, or union. (*Plate* 1.)

The Line of Marriage *Plate* 1 The Line of Marriage *Plate* 2 The Line of Marriage *Plate* 3

When this line curves downwards towards the palm, it foretells the death of the marriage partner. (*Plate* 2.)

When divided like a fork on the inside of the hand, it indicates separation, but not divorce. (*Plate* 3.)

When the fork-like appearance is shown on the outside, difficulties, delay and separation will occur before marriage.

When the Line of Marriage curves downwards in a fork with a line crossing to the ball of the thumb, divorce is indicated to the person on whose hand this mark appears. (*Plate* 4.)

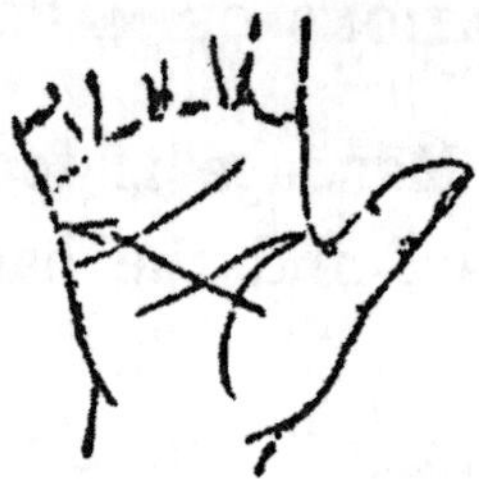

The Line of Marriage
Plate 4

When the Line of Marriage cuts downwards through the Line of Success, the subject will lose position and riches by marriage. (*Plate* 5.)

The Line of Marriage
Plate 5

The Line of Marriage
Plate 6

The Line of Marriage ending in a fork with a line from it joining the Line of Heart and the latter curving downwards, indicates a very unhappy marriage—but due to the exacting nature of the person on whose hand it appears. In this case there may never be separation or divorce, but it threatens a violent end to the marriage—death by violence is usually the verdict of the Jury. (*Plate* 6.)

The Line of Marriage with a line from it running into the Line of Head indicates that unhappiness and disputes will be caused by the

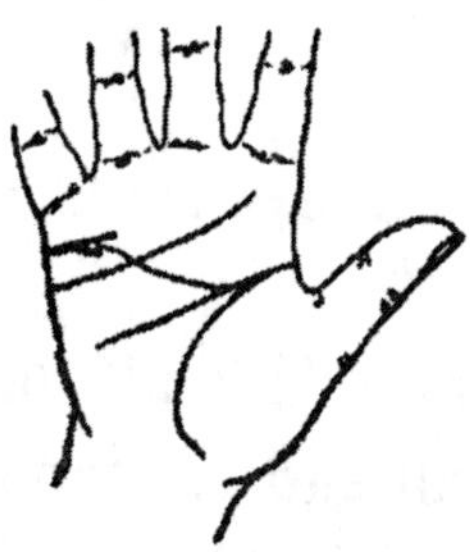

The Line of Marriage
Plate 7

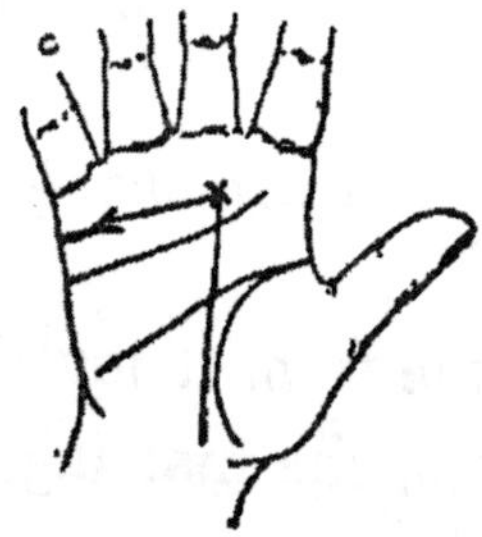

The Line of Marriage
Plate 8

opposition of the mental views of the partners as in the case of different religions marrying together. (*Plate* 7.)

If the Line of Marriage ends in a cross on the Line of Fate under the second finger, the marriage will terminate on the gallows. (*Plate* 8.)

When the Line of Marriage forms into an "island" and curves downward some tragedy or great sorrow such as long illness will end the life of the partner. (*Plate* 9.)

If a fine line is seen from the Line of Marriage going upwards into the Line of Success under the third finger, marriage will bring success, wealth and increase of position. (*Plate* 10.)

When the Line of Marriage terminates in a fork

The Line of Marriage
Plate 9

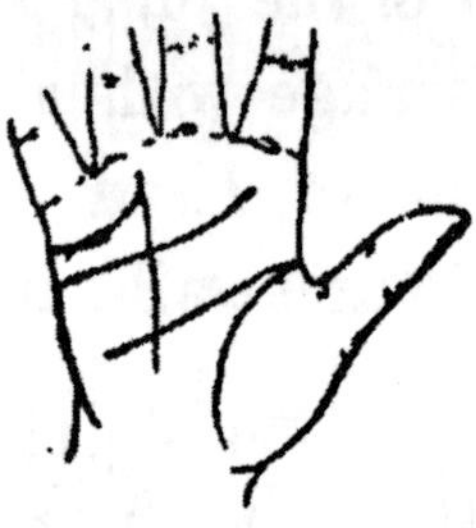

The Line of Marriage
Plate 10

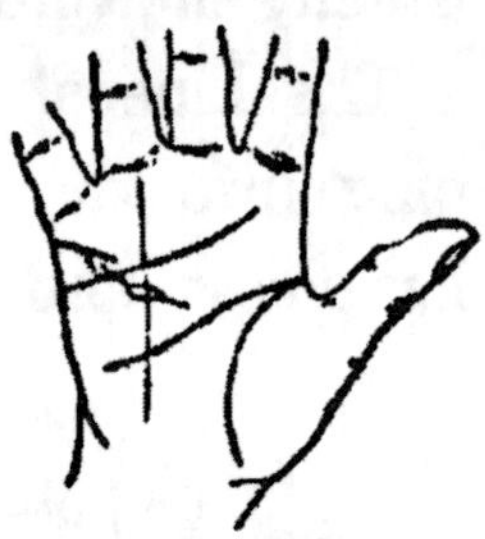

The Line of Marriage
Plate 11

with a line from it forming an "island" on the Line of Success, the marriage will end in scandal, loss of position and disgrace. (*Plate* 11.)

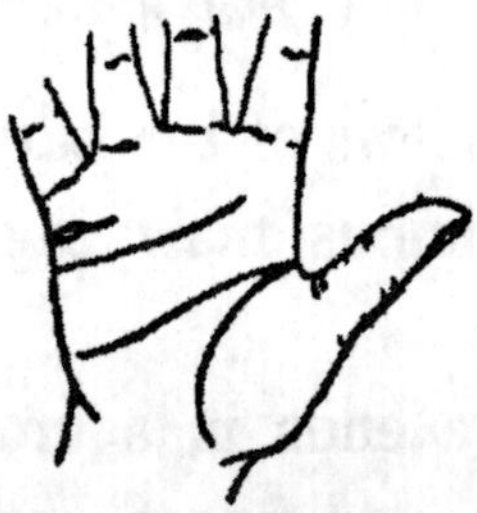

The Line of Marriage
Plate 12

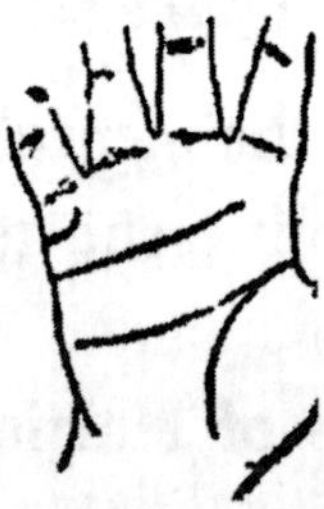

The Line of Marriage
Plate 13

The Line of Marriage starting with an "island" denotes seduction and trouble caused by it before marriage. If the line continues straight and clear, all will end well. (*Plate* 12.)

When the Line of Marriage is very short and curves upwards at the end, marriage is not likely to take place at any time. (*Plate* 13.)

The age when marriage will occur is indicated by the position of this line; the nearer to the Line of Heart, the earlier will be the marriage. (*Plate* 14.)

The date is further confirmed and more details often given by "Influence Lines" to the Line of Fate. (*Plate* 15.)

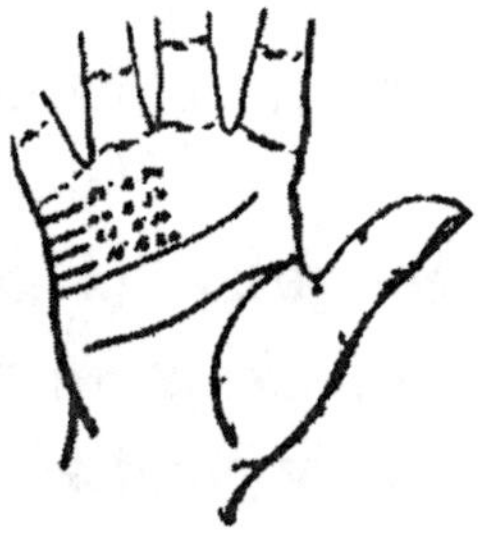

The Line of Marriage
Plate 14

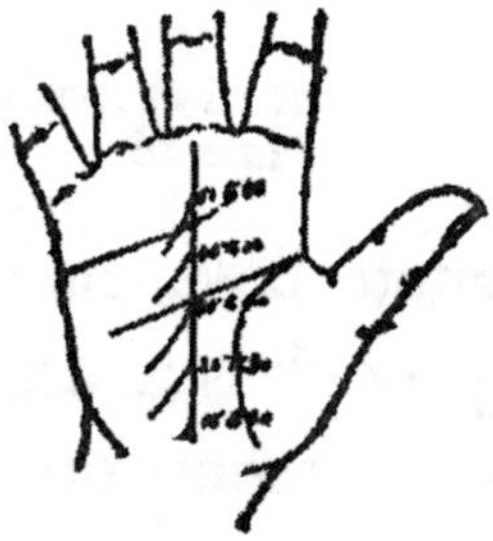

The Line of Marriage
Plate 15

Marriage or union is also shown by "Influence Lines" joining the Line of Fate. By the changes in the appearance of the latter after the junction of the line the result or effect of the union or marriage may be deduced.

If the Line of Fate appears stronger from the date where the "Influence Line" joins it, the union or marriage will have brought success. If fainter or broken up in "islands" or pieces, then the union or marriage has brought failure and ill-luck. (*Plate* 16.)

Children are indicated by fine but decided small lines that rise out of the Line of Marriage; strong

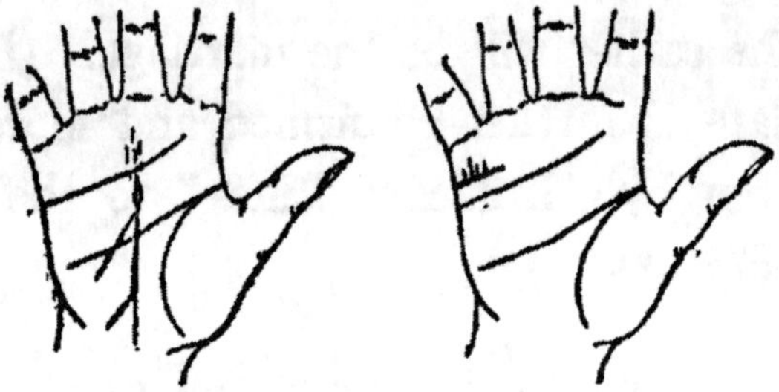

The Line of Marriage *Plate* 16 The Line of Marriage *Plate* 17

lines denote boys, fine lines, girls. (*Plate* 17.) A magnifying glass is useful in looking for these indications; after some practice very great accuracy can be obtained.

FURTHER REMARKS ON THE LINE OF MARRIAGE

It is a strange thing that amongst the many books written on the Study of the Hand, these lines should be to a great extent ignored or barely mentioned.

I consider them not only of the greatest possible interest in determining the future, but also of the greatest importance as a decisive argument in favour of Cheiromancy as regards dates, deaths, troubles and all events relating to marriage.

What is known as the Line of Marriage is the horizontal line or lines, as the case may be, on the Mount under the fourth finger. It may rise on the side of the hand, or be only marked across the face of the Mount.

The long lines only relate to marriage, the short ones deep affection, or of marriage contemplated. On the Line of Fate we can in many cases find the marriage corroborated, and information given as to the change of life, position, etc., brought about by the marriage and consequently the date when such an event takes place.

It will be noticed from the preceding Plates that from the position of the line on the Mount under the fourth finger, a very fair idea of age at the time of marriage may be ascertained.

To gain a close idea of the date, the best plan is to watch the Line of Fate, either for a change in one's position, or for a fine line running parall with it.

An important union or marriage is given by line rising from the Mount of Luna, and joining t Line of Fate, especially if the Fate Line lo stronger from this point or *if a Line of Sun begins for the first time.*

When the Line of Marriage on the Mou Mercury is distinct but with fine hair lines dro from it, it denotes trouble brought on by illness on the opposite side.

When the end of the line droops or curves downward towards the Line of Heart, it tells that the person with whom the subject is connected will die first. When the line curves upwards, the possessor is not likely to marry at any time.

When the line has an island in the centre, or at any portion, it foretells some heavy trouble in the married life—a separation of some kind, but not by law.

When the line divides into a drooping fork towards the Line of Heart, it tells of divorce or judicial separation. This is all the more certain if a fine line cross the hand from the fork in the Line of Marriage.

When the line breaks in two and curves downwards, it foretells the sudden death of the person connected with the subject. When the Line of larriage sends an offshoot on the Mount of the un, or to the Sun Line, it promises that its posses- r will marry someone of distinction or public sition.

When, on the contrary, the line cuts downwards reaks the Line of Sun, the person on whose it appears will lose position through marriage. en there is a short line running parallel and almost touching the Marriage Line, it tells of some deep affection, after marriage, on the side of the person on whose hand it appears.

In my larger books, "Cheiro's Language of the Hand" and "Cheiro's Guide to the Hand," also "Cheiro's Palmistry for All," I have been able to give more details on this portion of the subject that are impossible to give in a book of this size.

CHAPTER VIII

THE GIRDLE OF VENUS

THE Girdle of Venus is generally found as a kind of semi-circle rising between the first and second fingers, and ending between the third and fourth. (*Plate* 18.)

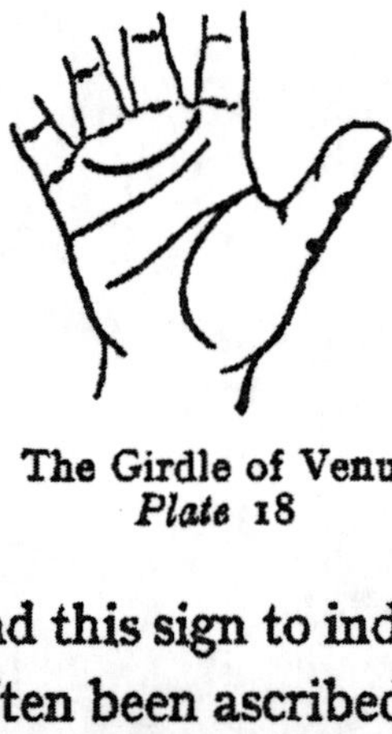

The Girdle of Venus
Plate 18

I have not found this sign to indicate the debauchery that has so often been ascribed to it, and simply, I believe on account of its name. On the contrary, I consider it to be associated with highly intellectual natures, but changeable in moods and extra sensitive. It also shows a highly-strung nervous temperament, to which this formation gives an unhappy tendency to hysteria and despondency.

People possessed with this mark are capable of rising to the highest pitch of enthusiasm, but are rarely twice in the same mood, one moment full of high spirits, and the next miserable and despondent.

When the Girdle goes over the side of the hand, particularly if it comes in contact with the Marriage Line under the fourth finger, it is rather against the happiness of the marriage, as the possessor would want as many virtues in a wife as there are stars in the universe.

CHAPTER IX

THE SYSTEM OF SEVEN

HOW TO TELL TIME AND DATES OF EVENTS

THE System of Seven (*Plate* 19) which I evolved from ancient records which were placed at my disposal, and from long experience in my own professional work, is, I consider the simplest and clearest method of calculating when the principal events or changes in one's career have taken place or are likely to take place.

This system is founded on the well-known natural law that the entire body in a measure changes every seven years.

From Medical Science we learn that there are seven distinct changes in the existence before birth, that the brain in its development takes seven forms before it takes "the unique character of the human brain," and that the entire system changes every seven years.

I have also found that as a general rule, the alternate seven years of life are somewhat alike in relations to the changes in the health of the body. For

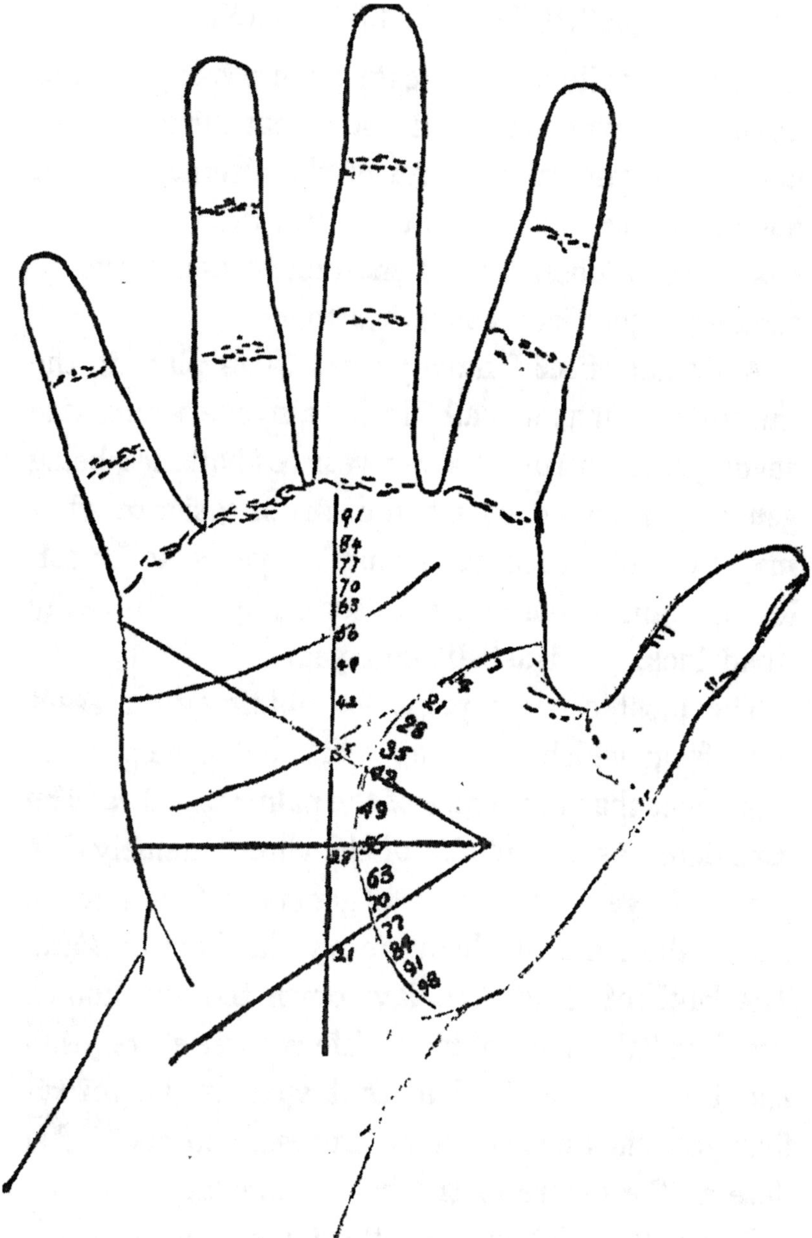

TIME—THE SYSTEM OF SEVEN

Plate 19

example, a child very delicate when passing the end of the first seven years will also repeat the same delicacy when passing the end of the alternate seven, such as between the twentieth and the twenty-first year. Such observations materially assist one in making predictions about health.

A similar effect I have proved takes place in the question of what we call "luck" also every alternate seven years. A run of seven years of bad luck being generally followed by a run of seven easier or what may be called good or favourable years, to be followed again in the alternate seven, by, if not really "bad luck," at least difficult years.

The most distinct point for obtaining an exact date from which one may work out others, is to remember that the centre of the palm may always be considered as the middle of the career, namely—35 years of age. This point is generally found to be where the Line of Head *crosses* the Line of Fate. The Book of Holy Writ lays down the well-known law that "the span of man's life is three score years and ten," and as half of that span is the thirty-fifth year the hand bears out this law and places this date as the centre of the human Destiny.

The most celebrated of the Greek philosophers, such as Anaxagoras and Aristotle, in following out this study, called the portion of the palm between the years twenty-one and thirty-five, "The Plain of Mars," or symbolic of the most difficult part of the fight in the "Battle of Life." These years thus become in the hand the two sides of the triangle as shown in the accompanying illustration, and a line drawn from the apex of this triangle cutting through the Line of Fate gives us the twenty-eighth year. Once these principal dates are clearly established, it becomes quite easy for the student to fill in the other years.

For still further particulars as to the method of arriving at still closer data, I must refer the reader to my larger books published on the Study of the Hand, especially "Cheiro's Palmistry for All," a very inexpensive work, but one that gives a wealth of information not published in any other books on the subject.

CHAPTER X

THE THUMB

THE Thumb (*Plate* 20), I must treat separately. I hold it to be one of the most important guides in the study of the hand.

From it you can tell with a glance the method of working, the character and disposition of the subject. Among gipsies, it is the first thing they look at; it gives them an insight at once into the lives of those with whom they come in contact; it is a solid foundation for all their remarks and suppositions. In India, it is also regarded as supreme, and great attention is paid to its position, shape, power, angle, and curves.

From the earliest ages we find the thumb playing an important part. Among Christian rites and ceremonies, it is even used to represent God, the episcopal blessing being given with the thumb and two first fingers only, the three representing Trinity, the thumb God, the all powerful.

It will also be observed that when children are born the thumb is invariably covered with the fingers, and it is a generally admitted fact that if a

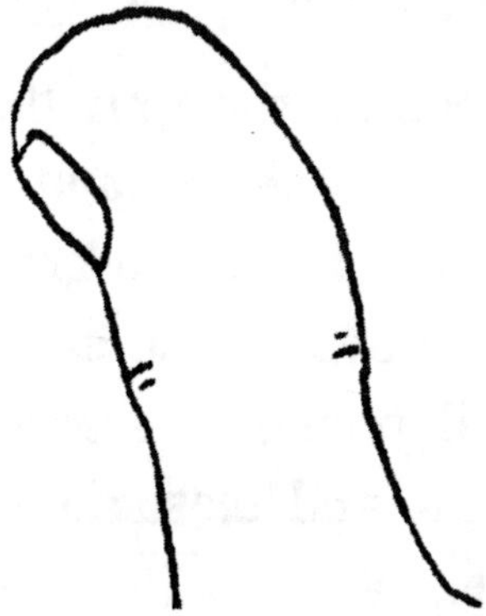

THE CLUBBED THUMB

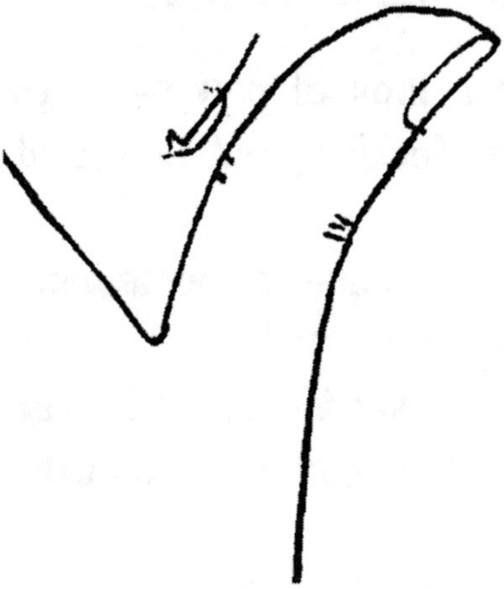

SUPPLE-JOINTED THUMB

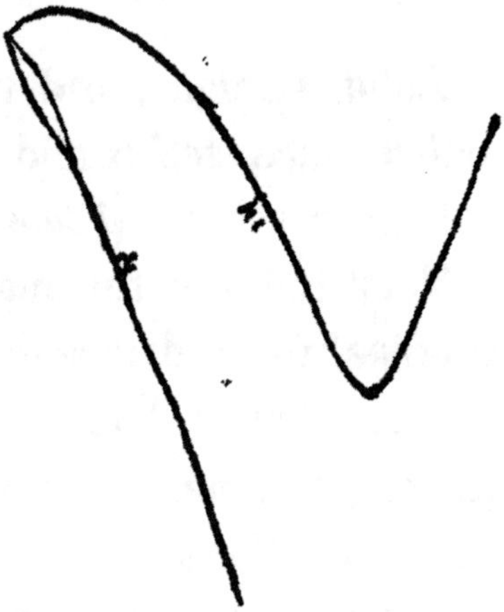

FIRM-JOINTED THUMB

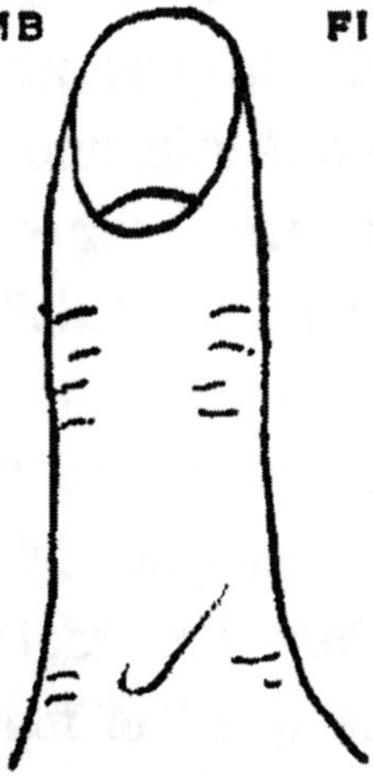

child persists in keeping the thumb covered it is a sure sign of delicacy—mental and physical. The thumb also represents the three great powers that control the world—Love, Logic and Will.

The first, or nail phalange—represents Will.

The second—Logic and reasoning power.

The third—Love.

FIRST PHALANGE (OR NAIL PHALANGE)

Long, straight, and with a look of power—gives self-reliance, self-confidence, decision and power of will over others. (*Plate* 20.)

Very full and turning backwards—extravagance, prodigality, and generosity. (*Plate* 20.)

Flat, thin and turning backwards—control over temper, calmness, strong decision and great adaptability to others.

Very pointed, full and turning backwards—great impulsiveness and extravagant ideas.

When the thumb is stiff and straight in the first joint, the subjects are inclined to be dogged and obstinate. They find it difficult to suit themselves to either people or surroundings; they lead their own way—let those follow who will. They are not so suave in manner as people with the thumb turning backward, but they are more reliable in their promises and more silent in manner.

When the first phalange curves and turns inwards, the subject is niggardly and miserly in money matters; very cautious and suspicious, distrustful of people and things, and reserved and distant in manner.

When this phalange is small and weak it denotes inconstancy, changeability, vacillation. The subjects are easily influenced by others; they never make reliable friends, as they are always ready to be dominated by a stronger will.

The "Clubbed Thumb" (*Plate* 20) is a sign of violent temper; when roused, persons with this class of thumb "see red," and often commit murder in a fit of passion.

SECOND PHALANGE

When this phalange is long, and heavy, the subject will reason out every step of his life, but, if this phalange is longer than the first, he will not have the will, power and decision necessary to carry out his plans or ideas. He would, however, be excellent at giving counsel or advice to others.

When the two phalanges are equal in length the subject is strong in will-power and sensible in ideas, just and honourable, and would rule without tyranny.

When the second phalange is thick and clumsy, the subject though having good plans and ideas, will, from want of tact, find them difficult in execution. He might not be aggressive, but he would offend people by his manner and way of putting things. He would say and do awkward things, and would be continually getting into trouble with friends.

On the other hand, when this phalange is beautifully shaped and formed like a waist, it gives great diplomacy and tact, often great deceitfulness. It is seen in the hands of diplomatists and the pets of Society. These people have always the power of getting themselves out of difficulties. (*Plate* 20.)

THIRD PHALANGE

The proper place to consider this phalange is, lying outside the Mount of Venus, below the second and running downwards to the wrist.

When long, clear, and angular in shape, love leans to the ideal. It is regarded more as a sacred idea of the soul than anything vulgar, earthly or sensual.

When it is short and clumsy, love is a passion. It requires, at all times, some positive assurance that the liking is reciprocated. It gives passion and asks for passion in return. When this development has a full and heavily-marked Mount of Venus by its side, we then find the sensual tendency of the nature accentuated.

Measure the thumb with the first finger—the higher it goes, the higher the intellectual capacity of the subject. If you wish to examine and prove this closer, take, as a starting point, the hand of a monkey (the nearest approach to the human species)—you will find here that the top of the thumb hardly comes within touch of the root of the first finger, and if you go farther and examine the hands of intellectual men, against those who lead a more animal and vegetable life, you will find the higher the mental development the higher and longer the thumb.

When the thumb is well developed with the first phalange, denoting power, and the little finger long, you get at once the dispositions that crave for power and authority. They can always influence people so that they may obtain their desires. This development gives great success in a public or a diplomatic life.

CHAPTER XI

THE NAILS

I CONSIDER the nails (*Plate* 21) most important in the study of the hand—they are sure indications of temper, and also of health.

Large, round nails, bluish in colour, tell of weak action of the heart and bad circulation, especially if the "moon" is very small.

Thin nails denote delicate health.

Long, fluted nails, particularly if wide and curved towards the top, are indicators of consumption. (*Plate* 21.)

Short round nails go with a tendency for throat and bronchial troubles. (*Plate* 21.)

Paralysis is indicated when the nails are shell-shaped, pointed at the base and very small. (*Plate* 22.)

As indicators of character, short nails, well formed, give criticism and contradiction—and if more decidedly marked on the third finger, they give mimicry and wit. Large nails, wide at the bottom, are careful and good in business.

Filbert nails are kind, sweet-tempered and forgiving.

Large nails always show more calmness and resignation than the short type.

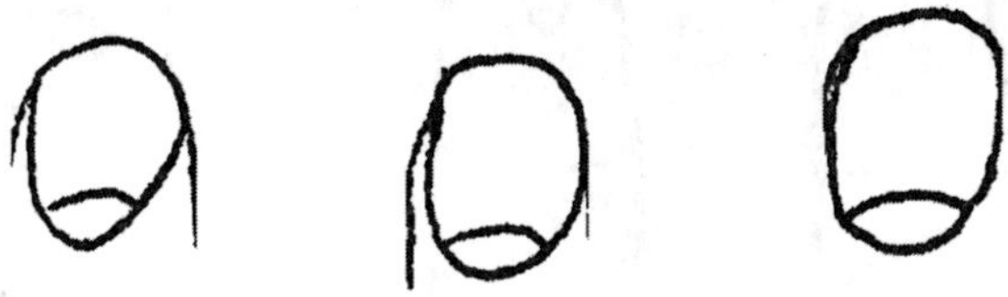

THROAT AFFECTIONS AND BRONCHIAL

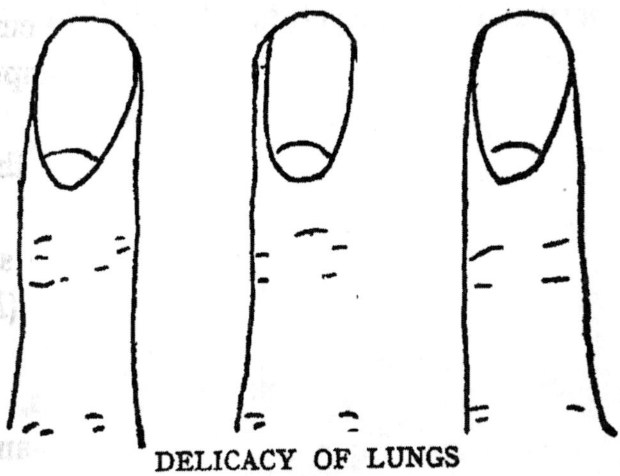

DELICACY OF LUNGS

Plate 21

Short-nailed people are usually good critics, they are quicker at seizing and bringing out those details which might, and would, escape the long-nailed people. Short-nailed people are hard to beat in

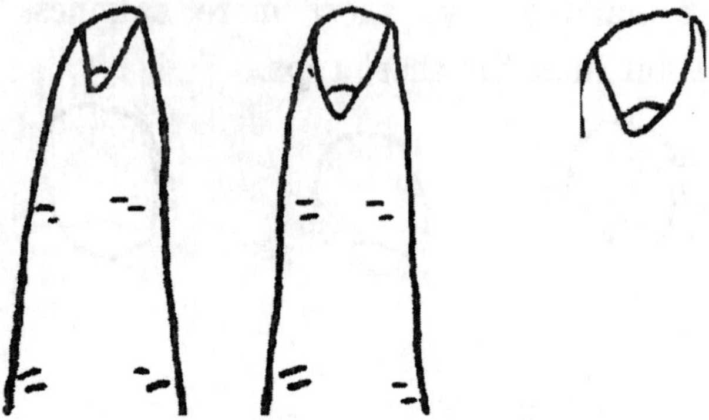

SHOWING TENDENCY TOWARDS PARALYSIS
Plate 22

debate; the long-nailed people are more idealistic, more artistic in temperament and more enthusiastic over work and the things that interest them.

CHAPTER XII

CONCLUSION

AS I have completely retired from all professional work, I have taken the opportunity of the Cinema and of this low-priced book to reach the widest possible section of the public, in order that the world at large may have the means of making use of—what I believe to be—a study that can be *of the greatest benefit to humanity.*

By the knowledge that I am thus enabled to "broadcast" far and wide, I am convinced that thousands and perhaps hundreds of thousands of my fellow-beings will be able to take advantage of the long years I have devoted to this study and derive *practical help* and benefit from it.

On the Cinema I have been able to show the impressions from real hands to illustrate the various rules I have given in this book. In order to do this I have used the hands of such well-known persons. (who gave me autographed impressions) as the Grand Old Man of England—Gladstone; The Right Hon. Joseph Chamberlain; The Right Hon

Sir Austen Chamberlain; the famous explorer, Sir H. M. Stanley, who was sent across Africa to find Livingstone; Lord Russell of Killowen, Lord Chief Justice of England; the famous King's Counsel, Sir Edward Marshall Hall; Prince Louis Napoleon; Bernhardt; Melba; Calvé; Mrs. Langtry and many others.

On account of the size of this book, I am unable to reproduce these hands in its pages, but readers who are interested in pursuing this study further will find these autographed impressions, together with fuller details, in my "Language of the Hand," and other works I have published and which they can easily obtain from all book-sellers.

"CHEIRO."

FINIS.